THE RISE OF THE AMBIDEXTROUS ORGANIZATION

The Secret Revolution
Happening Right Under Your Nose

BY ERIC ZABIEGALSKI, ED.D.

Printed in the United States of America
ISBN 978-1-64633-341-7 Paperback
ISBN 978-1-64633-340-0 Ebook

"Every once in a while, a book comes around that informs and unites us. This is such a book. The author turns what might seem an esoteric business topic into a highly relatable search for balance and inclusion that benefits us all. Dr. Zabiegalski has written what should be required reading for every leader, entrepreneur, educator, and manager."
—**Timothy Lucente, Solutions Consultant**

"At the leading edge of a global phenomenon, Dr. Zabiegalski is a pathfinder on the subject of organizational ambidexterity. Dr. Eric's book places us squarely at the intersection of thought and practice by offering pragmatic approaches to understand, thrive, and fuel meaningful paradigm shifts in this dynamically connected complex world." —**Thomas Kleiner, Ph.D., Executive in Residence, Webster University**

"Eric paints a vivid picture of how to build tomorrow's successful organizations, where team members feel safe to dream, create, question the status quo, take risks, and ultimately find fulfillment. If you're ready to join the movement, this book is for you!" —**Bob Chapman, CEO, Barry-Wehmiller; author of** *Everybody Matters: The Extraordinary Power of Caring for Your People Like Family*

"Between the pages of this book are lessons that transcend business as usual. Inclusion, diversity, empathy, and newly realized, fulfilling performance, it is Eastern consciousness meets Western pragmatism." —**Dr. Arun Manilal Gandhi, Sociopolitical Activist, Senior Practitioner, Bosserman Center for Conflict Resolution, Salisbury University, and Fifth Grandson of Mohandas Gandhi**

"As I read this excellent book, three companies kept coming into my mind: Kodak, Blockbuster, and Blackberry. The failure of these organizations to develop explorative processes and mindsets is a powerful illustration of why the concepts laid out in this highly effective guidebook should be embraced. *The Rise of the AO* is a thoroughly enjoyable read which deserves to do well!" —**Martin Lister, Humanintelligence, Inc., United Kingdom**

"Eric has done a masterful job dissecting what makes an organization tick and excel! As a founder and owner of a rapidly growing 100-person high-tech company, I found that the descriptions and concepts presented in Eric's book are thought provoking and hit close to home. Leadership is a complex art form that constantly needs to change and evolve. Eric describes this rewarding challenge brilliantly in a clear, concise, easy-to-understand manner." —**Mike Bechtold, President, OptiPro Systems**

"The challenges in leading a large organization responsible for rapid prototyping, rapid fielding, and accelerating innovative technology are massive and complex. Dr. Zabiegalski has provided a comprehensive and insightful framework that allows a leadership team to successfully balance an organization's cultural extremes and leverage them with ambidextrous energy to drive to continued success! An absolute must read for any leader who wants a balanced and meaningful approach for positive organizational change." —**Gerald Swift, Director, AIRWorks, Naval Air Warfare Center Aircraft Division**

"All leaders struggle with the balance between exploitive leadership practices (supporting traditional work) and explorative leadership (supporting innovation and creativity) to win in the future. Success in the present, and future, is a leadership responsibility and imperative. Eric's current work on ambidextrous leadership will enrich the minds of leadership practitioners for decades to come." —**Don Bacon, Congressman, Nebraska's 2nd District**

"Many organizations focus on innovation, new products and services, while others continue to exploit the products and services they already have. In *Rise of the AO*, Eric discusses the challenges and benefits for organizations that can do both. Addressing the primary challenges ambidextrous organizations face, especially cultural change, this is an essential guide for any company wanting to become ambidextrous." —**William Thoet, Retired EVP, Booz Allen Hamilton, Former Chairman of the ALS Association, Owner of Georgetown Piano Bar**

"An over-the-horizon thinker, Dr. Zabiegalski addresses the tough cultural and sociological phenomena we can no longer ignore if we want to advance in work and wellness for the 21st century. Outlining the construct of organizational ambidexterity, Eric illustrates how this behavioral model is more than a shrewd business strategy; it's a template for living and working your best life!" —**Brian Polkinghorn, Ph.D., Executive Director, Bosserman Center for Conflict Resolution, Salisbury University**

"Dr. Zabiegalski has written the most comprehensive work on the subject of organizational ambidexterity I have ever read! Don't know what an ambidextrous organization is? Then this is the must read, especially if you work in organizational development." —**Tomasz Janiak, Master Action Learning Coach, WIAL Poland**

"Learning never stops! Dr. Zabiegalski shines a light on the concept of organizational ambidexterity and the importance of organizations investing in their employees and a culture of learning and establishing a flexible structure that creates opportunities for success. A "must read" for every agile organization!"—**Oscar Barrow, Program Management Professional**

"Dr Z's business sense is spot on! It's do or die on the field of business, and those that don't reach out to create new markets will not survive. Every time I read this book I learn." —**Kevin Rosser, Engineer, TRC Corp.**

"In this ever-changing world of new techniques and methods to continued company growth, Eric puts forth an inventive approach as to why companies and people do what they do. This is a thought-provoking book!" —**James Morton, CEO/President, GTMR Inc.**

"Being creative and innovative yet also executing to perfection: While these are often seen as opposites of a spectrum, every organization needs both to be successful. Eric explores the world of ambidextrous organizations and pulls on a rich array of references and models to show how both can be achieved, at the same time, all the time! He offers food for thought and concrete ideas to put in place to reach the ultimate 'ambidextrous organization.'" —**Peter Cauwelier, WIAL Thailand**

"Outstanding read professionally and personally! Dr. Zabiegalski presents dynamic, well-written, and timely research. There is value in organizational awareness and caution to be taken in the quest for market exploitation at the expense of exploration, which promotes new ideas and fresh opportunities!" —**Will Jones, Program Manager, NAVAIR**

"*The Rise of the Ambidextrous Organization* is an inventive look at guiding organizations exploratively and exploitatively to self-actualize within the office and the marketplace. With precision, Zabiegalski takes apart the cultural, leadership, and environmental engines of an organization, describes each component, and shows how ambidextrous leaders provide value to any organization." —**Mike Sundsted, Former Air Force One Pilot, Motivational Speaker**

"*The Rise of the Ambidextrous Organization* offers sage advice for leaders striving to impact their organization's learning culture in a positive way. Eric's enlightening work will be of particular interest to anyone using agile approaches to organizations and teams." —**Paddy Corry, Scrum Master, Dublin, Ireland**

"Dr. Zabiegalski does a magnificent job leading the reader through a difficult topic using sound references and life experiences. Humans avoid change, but in this book, Dr. Z inspires readers to never stop learning, referencing experiences and failures to minimize risk. A masterpiece written by a professional leading by example!" —**Steve Dallaire, Retired U.S. Navy F/A-18 Pilot, Squadron Commander, Navy Topgun Weapons School Graduate, Blue Angels Super Hornet Transition Support Team**

"Dr. Zabiegalski details how to lead and manage complex business environments. Do you want a thriving organization in today's complex environment, one that can manage disorder and chaos while keeping an eye on the future? Then this book is for you!" —**Eric Gafford, Aerospace Publications Supervisor**

"So much of coaching revolves around challenging the fears conjured up by the mind. Dr. Zabiegalski addresses these beautifully in *The Rise of the Ambidextrous Organization* when he advises readers to "know what part of your brain is giving you advice." We couldn't have said it better ourselves! —**The Heart Wants Adventure, Professional Life Coaching Services**

"Dr. Eric Zabiegalski's book, *The Rise of the Ambidextrous Organization*, is a valuable addition to organizational literature about companies and their internal processes. To use a flying analogy, AOs use a scan pattern like pilots to ensure they don't fixate on one variable while ignoring others. If I stare at my airspeed indicator, blocking out other instruments, I may not notice that I'm descending. Altimeter, airspeed, attitude, course— successful pilots and successful companies keep their scan moving, giving more attention to the instruments that need it, but never letting their focus become fixation. This skill requires practice and repetition. Dr. Z provides the cues to keep an organization's scan moving and (organizationally speaking) keep the blue side up!" —**Michael W. Eaton, Former Air Force 2 Pilot, Captain at a Major U.S. Airline**

"A refreshing perspective on organizational learning! Dr. Eric Zabiegalski captures the vital elements to building and sustaining a winning organization in today's highly complex and ultra-competitive environment. A perfect blend of science and leadership theory, this book is packed with transcendent, actionable advice to help leaders shape a culture of innovative, resilient, and agile thinkers—focused on advancing the fighting edge by harnessing the power of the *ambidextrous mindset.*" —**Kristofer Reyes, Director, Talent Management and Organizational Learning, U.S. Air Force**

Table of Contents

Preface

When Dr. Michael Marquardt agreed to write the foreword to *The Rise of the Ambidextrous Organization*, I was "over the moon"; I couldn't be happier. Professor Marquardt—co-founder and first president of the World Institute for Action Learning (WIAL), who now serves as chair of the WIAL Advisory Committee and head of The George Washington University doctoral program for human and organizational learning—was my dissertation chair for that program. As an action learning coach, Mike has trained more than 100,000 managers in over 170 countries with consulting assignments including Marriott, Microsoft, Sony Music, Goodrich, Motorola, Nortel, Alcoa, Boeing, Caterpillar, United Nations Development Program, Xerox, Nokia, Constellation, Samsung, Organization of American States, and Singapore Airlines, as well as the governments of Indonesia, Laos, Ethiopia, Zambia, Egypt, Kuwait, Saudi Arabia, Turkey, Russia, Jamaica, Honduras, and Swaziland.

Mike has also authored 26 books and over 100 professional articles in the fields of leadership, learning, globalization, and organizational change. His books include *Action Learning for Developing Leaders and Organizations, Optimizing the Power of Action Learning, Leading with Questions,* and *Building the Learning Organization* (selected as Book of the Year by the Academy of Human Resource Development). Over 1 million copies of his publications have been sold in over a dozen languages worldwide. He's served as the editor of the UNESCO encyclopedia volume on human resources, is an editor and/or advisor for several leading professional journals around the world, and has been a keynote speaker at international conferences in Australia, Japan, Philippines, Malaysia, South Africa, Singapore, and India as well as throughout North America.

In addition to these accomplishments (and counting), Mike has also been a friend and mentor to me for 10 years. As senior instructor and head of GWU's human and organizational learning program and chair for my original research on ambidextrous organizations, Mike encouraged me to keep asking questions and reach for the improbable—and this advice made all the difference. Perhaps most transformative has been watching Mike coach action learning in organizations as they simultaneously *build high-performing teams, develop leaders* of everyone in the room, and find *breakthrough strategies* for the urgent problem facing the group. When all the rules and components are in place, the action learning process is like a magic card trick; it works every time. It's electric to watch an action learning group have a breakthrough and begin performing as a team (often for the first time even among teams that have worked together for years). Action learning truly changes lives.

The connection between learning and the ambidextrous organization is strong. Bottom line: If you don't have a learning organization, you won't achieve ambidexterity. Learning is present in both exploitative and explorative activities, albeit in different incarnations, and now more than ever it's of the utmost importance to make room at the C-suite table for a learning leader who will champion all forms of learning. Learning needs to have an equal place alongside performance if humanity wants to achieve continued success and prosperity. Right from the beginning, when I brought the idea of making organizational ambidexterity the focus of my research, Mike was supportive and saw the importance of studying, developing, and encouraging both *exploitative* and *explorative* learning within organizations.

Foreword

In the 1970s and 1980s, the twin forces of globalization and technology changed the world of work and catapulted organizations into a new era, an era in which neither industrial- nor knowledge-based institutions were able to change as fast as the environment around them. Learning to become a learning organization became ever more critical. Soon, companies such as Shell, Singapore Airlines, Federal Express, and Whirlpool began this journey.

Peter Senge made the concept of learning organizations popular with his bestselling book *The Fifth Discipline*, which was published in 1990. That book was quickly followed by learning organization books authored by leading scholars such as Pedler, Burgoyne, and Boydell[1] and Watkins and Marsick.[2] As a professor and a member of the Organizational Learning Center at George Washington University, I joined the conversation in 1994 with *The Global Learning Organization*. Over the past 25 years, I continued my research with several books on learning organizations as well as books on action learning, which I discovered was the most effective way of building a learning organization.

With this remarkable book, *The Rise of the Ambidextrous Organization*, Eric Zabiegalski has made a magnificent and significant contribution to the learning organization field. His

---

[1] Pedler, M., Burgoyne, J., & Boydell, T. (1991, 1997). *The learning company*. https://www. amazon.com/gp/product/0077093003/ref=dbs_a_def_rwt_bibl_vppi_i1

[2] Watkins, K. E., & Marsick, V. J. (1993). *Sculpting the learning organization: Lessons in the art and science of systemic change*. https://www.amazon.com/gp/product/B01A68498Y/ref=dbs_a_def_rwt_bibl_vppi_i0

insight that learning organizations must be both exploitative (build and expand on their existing products and services) and explorative (continue to create new products and services) is a truly valuable addition to the growing literature on learning organizations. As he notes, very few organizations are strong in both exploitation and exploration; those that are (e.g., Google) have a tremendous advantage in the work world of the 21st century.

In this book, Eric not only describes why ambidextrous organizations are so important, but also provides powerful ideas and insights on the process and steps in building such an organization. It's a wonderful book, and I highly recommend it to anyone who is seeking to build an organization that can lead and learn in a turbulent world.

Dr. Zabiegalski is the rare scholar-practitioner who has the ability to incorporate cutting-edge theories such as complexity, psychology, philosophy, management science, action learning, and economics with his many years as a successful leader and consultant. This book captures his wisdom and common sense, which results in pages of great ideas and even greater recommendations on how the reader can build an ambidextrous learning organization.

—MICHAEL J. MARQUARDT
Professor Emeritus, George Washington University
Co-founder, World Institute for Action Learning

1

Introduction

ere's the bottom line regarding learning and organizations: Research into formerly high performing organizations has consistently found that *organizational exploitation drives out exploration.* What does that mean? It's simple: As organizations exploit the marketplace by doing what they do best for profit and market share, they consequently stop exploring and looking for new ideas; they stop learning in critical ways that could guarantee future success. It's not hard to do in companies, if you think about it. For one thing, it's difficult to do two things at once, particularly if those two things appear to conflict with one another or be un-related, requiring different thinking and acting. Secondly, there always seems to be some other "alligators close to the boat" that need immediate swatting before you can even think about explor-ing, being creative, or learning anything new. Companies that adopt this exploitation lather, rinse, and repeat mindset, however, risk losing the balance they once had between everyday perfor-mance and innovative creativity and the ability to leverage learning in new ways that guarantee sustained long-term success. To put this performance strategy into a sports metaphor, they're setting themselves up for a great short game but no long one!

Key

The Solution of Ambidexterity

If 40-plus years of research about exploitation and exploration says this is an inevitable dilemma, and it does, then what's the solution? The solution is the practice of *organizational ambidexterity,* the ability to be simultaneously exploitative and explorative in the marketplace, managing both elements in a rhythmic balance and dance that promote both short- and long-term performance and success. Mastering ambidexterity is not easy and takes a certain amount of trust and grit; however, for the companies that adopt this model and routinely execute it, like Toyota and Google, it is a combination that works and works well.

Organizations seldom consider their historical behavior and are often unaware of the evolutionary changes that led them into this success trap of continually favoring exploitation over exploration. Some companies feel as though they lack the resources, knowledge, or ability to risk growing through exploration, while others fall into a pattern perpetuated by *cultural* or *structural* inertia, becoming too resistant to change either by norms, stories, and company rules (culture) or by having an organizational business structure that is too rigid to adopt anything but the smallest of changes (structural). When this happens, the organizations effectively become a "one-trick pony." So, what does it take to have an ambidextrous organization—an AO?

Definitions

Before we dive into the types of organizational ambidexterity in an AO, let's cover a few definitions.

Exploitation is the refinement of existing knowledge within an organization's departments. It is associated with making existing improvements and incremental adjustments and increasing efficiency—in other words, it's the business of doing better what you have already learned to do.

Exploration, on the other hand, is the pursuit of new knowledge, which includes variety generation, distant search, risk taking, experimentation, and discovery. In other words, it's learning to do new things for the first time.

Organizational ambidexterity, then, is defined as the ability of an organization to both explore and exploit, to compete in mature technologies and markets where unique knowledge, efficiency, control, and incremental improvement are prized and in new technologies and markets where flexibility, autonomy, and experimentation are needed. By now it should be apparent that all these traits are great ones to have! Let's look at the three types of ambidexterity in practice today, but first let's review the AO model.

The Model

The ambidextrous organization model shows where all organizations go and where most stop. All organizations begin ambidextrously by either looking for or learning how to do something well. In this depiction, the company is "driving down," exploratively looking for products or trying to perfect the products it's chosen, exploit them, and dominate the market with them for profit. After a period of time, this is achieved, and the exploration practices turn to exploitation and the model flips. Now the company is almost exclusively driving down into exploitation—and, for most organizations, this is where the model ends.

There may be intermittent (passing) periods of exploration— i.e., the boss gets a new idea, an enthusiastic new employee pitches an innovative idea, or the annual company off-site happens, and people feel free to let their hair down and express their ideas freely

The ambidextrous organization model (Zabiegalski, 2015).

in this atmosphere. But ambidextrous organizations go beyond the dotted line in the model and the model changes one more time, this time internally. When this happens, the explorative part of the organization takes up residence permanently as the capstone of the organization while the exploitative processes become the foundation; each is respected and of equal stature and importance philosophically, and each feeds and supports the other. The explorative part of the company innovates and provides new competencies for the exploitative part, and the exploitative part tethers and resources the explorative, providing foundation and muse for it. What my research into ambidexterity told me was that experiencing ambidexterity was not rare; however, sustaining it was.

Three Types of Ambidexterity

The first type, *temporal ambidexterity*, is practiced by all organizations, whether they realize it or not. When you think of temporal ambidexterity, think about switching back and forth from exploitative to explorative behavior and back again at some specified time. If you're practicing temporal ambidexterity, your organization is taking a break from "converging," focusing intently on what it does best, and switching to "diverging" and widening the focus onto new things. Temporally ambidextrous practices might be your company picnic once a year or that team-building retreat you go to in the mountains. It might be an annual convention or anything the company endorses that encourages you to take in new learning and operate in less or differently structured spaces.

Structural ambidexterity, the next type, can be described as a separate "explorative" space created by the organization in which it is allowable to explore and be creative or innovative. To understand this type, think of any organization with a research and development department, advanced development division, or creative space. Examples of this include Disney's "DreamWorks" division or Lockheed Martin's famous aircraft "Skunkworks." A structurally

4

ambidextrous space is any designated space where it's permissible to be creative or innovative.

Our last type, _contextual ambidexterity_, is the most difficult type for an organization to achieve but arguably the best. It's safe to say that when you reach this level, you and your organization have _arrived_ as an AO. To understand contextual ambidexterity, think about biology at a cellular level. Ambidexterity, the ability to exploit and explore in appropriate amounts and at appropriate times, reaches your organization's culture down to the individual employee level. No "switching" rules (temporal ambidexterity) are required by the organization at this point, though they most likely still happen, and no specific explorative safe "space" (structural ambidexterity) is needed, though you may still have one. The whole organization functions as one productive and creative space as needed. This kind of ambidexterity gets into a company's DNA!

About This Book

To help you get the most from this book, it has been designed to take you on a journey, entertain you with stories, educate and stretch your current knowledge and thinking, and encourage you to reflect and question the world in which you live. Whether you read it once and put it down, bend pages and highlight passages, write in the margins as if you're having a conversation with it, use it as a desk reference, or leave it on the board room table of your West Coast office after reading it on the flight out, it matters little; if you read it, it will change you forever.

This book is divided into four parts. The first part discusses elements of AO: culture, leadership, learning, and structure. Afterwards, the environment of complexity is addressed, with discussions of the science of complexity, equilibrium, symmetry, structure, emergence, chaos, and governance. The third part presents strategies to help you cultivate an ambidextrous mind by overcoming some hurdles and being authentic. The book closes by describing how to arrive at organizational ambidexterity.

PART I:
THE ELEMENTS OF ORGANIZATIONAL AMBIDEXTERITY

2

Culture

What Is Organizational Culture?

Edgar Schein, a famous cultural researcher, once commented that "perhaps the single most important thing a leader does for their organization is set that organization's culture."[3] If you only accomplish this one task, then theoretically you will be guaranteed a great organization. I believe this theory whole-heartedly and would add that if you do not intentionally set your company culture, one will take shape anyway that you might not like or even understand. Since current academic thinking says it takes 7 years to change a company's culture, this can be a scary thought!

Organizational culture is a concept that represents the *beliefs, values, and assumptions* shared within an organization and has its roots in anthropology, sociology, psychology, and other social science disciplines. First hypothesized in the 1920s, it wasn't taken seriously by businesses until the 1970s and remains open to new interpretation and discovery today. There are still leaders who believe culture is pure bunk. There is no convincing these organizational "flat-earthers" otherwise (no offense to real flat-earthers). The rest of us, however, know that companies both contain and create cultures. So, what type of behaviors and practices are not compatible with an ambidextrous organization (AO) culture? Let's take a look.

---

[3] Organizational Culture and Leadership Institute. http://www.scheinocli.org/

Cultural Ambidexterity

As discussed in the introduction, there is one type of ambidexterity, *contextual*, that gets into a company's culture right down to its very DNA; we can refer to this type as *cultural ambidexterity.* To gain cultural ambidexterity, you must have a strong, aware, courageous, and caring leader with the heart of a teacher and learner (more on the ambidextrous leader in chapter 3). You must also begin with a healthy, open, and learning culture, as opposed to one whose members are stacking sand bags at their desks.

In her great article "How to Kill Creativity," researcher and writer Teresa Amabile said there are many unfortunate behaviors that kill the explorative, creative, or innovative side of organizations, i.e., that kill ambidexterity![4] Perhaps the best way of describing an ambidextrous culture is by telling you what it's not and what it *shouldn't* be. Here's a list built upon Teresa's research that may reveal the barriers to ambidexterity lurking in your hallways:

- Homogeneous teams
- Leaders and managers with little or no knowledge of their employees
- Criticality or negativity bias towards new ideas
- A climate of fear concerning the introduction of new ideas
- An organizational ecosystem that kills creativity
- Lack of a safety net for mistakes; lack of value placed on failure
- Little intrinsic motivation/only monetary reward systems (i.e., pay for performance)
- Lack of sharing problem-solving solutions
- Lack of valuing knowledge from disparate fields
- Lack of a place for slower learners to "explore the maze"
- No allowance for incubation
- Lack of thought given to job matching

---

[4] Amabile, T. (1998). How to kill creativity. *Harvard Business Review.* https://hbr.org/1998/09/how-to-kill-creativity

- Tight control of resources (when unnecessary)
- Poor use of physical space and lack of design considerations

Ask yourself objectively if you're suffering from any of these afflictions, keeping in mind the antithesis of these behaviors and practices shines a light on what a healthy AO culture looks like!

Attitude Counts

ATDT, or *attitude toward divergent thinking*, is the positive or negative attitude taken towards new experiences and thinking abstractly and creatively and significantly impacts an AO regarding exploration. If your company has an indifferent or negative attitude towards divergent thinking, you'll see individuals and processes promoting it being undervalued, ignored, marginalized, or even persecuted. Neurologically, most individuals are either data-driven, analytical, and objective (using the left hemisphere of the brain) or have an abstract, subjective, big-picture way of thinking (using the right hemisphere), so it's important for ambidextrous leaders to embrace being a "whole-brain" thinker as they influence their organization.

And So Does the Right Mindset

Carol Dweck, professor of psychology at Stanford University, is known for her work on mindset and psychological traits. She said that people adopt one of two mindsets: a fixed mindset or a growth mindset. She concluded that a growth mindset will allow a person to live a less stressful, more successful life. In her video on *learning mindsets* and the concept of *grit*, Dweck said talent doesn't build grit (an indomitable spirit and resolution in the face of difficulty), but having a *growth mindset* (vs. a fixed mindset) does. In her words, a fixed mindset says that the need to apply effort is a sign you don't have ability; effort, in effect, reveals you, and questions represent effort. Those who think that innate intelligence or talent is the driving force behind their success see no room for learning or improvement because "you either have ability or you don't."

Dweck said this is common in organizations, and she nicknamed it the "CEO disease." Those with a fixed mindset are often afraid to fail because they see it as an indictment of their intelligence and ability. As a result, they veer towards safer, predictable outcomes.

By contrast, a growth mindset says we learn at all times, and the ability to learn, and learning, is not fixed or a sign of deficiency. A growth mindset (grit) forces us out of our comfort zone and strengthens neurons in the brain. How do you develop grit and a growth mindset? Dweck said praise process vs. procedure or product and praise those "gritty" people who don't shy away from struggle.[5]

People, and organizations, are more likely to succeed if they have a growth mindset, believing that their most basic abilities can be developed through dedication and hard work and that complex problems or obstacles provide us learning opportunities. These are people who are willing to take on difficult issues because the outcome is not tied to their self-worth. According to Dweck, people who believe that success comes from effort are also more likely to rebound after failure. They are persistent, willing to try again because they believe that the failure stemmed from external factors or the need to apply more effort rather than from a fixed trait. Someone who sees failure as a result of not being smart enough is not motivated to try again after failing. This has important implications for organizations, which frequently must rebound from failure.

You can cultivate a growth mindset in employees by creating a culture that embraces learning. To do this, treat failures as learning opportunities by encouraging cooperation and ensuring that employees who pursue exploration efforts and fail are not subject to judgment or punishment but instead are celebrated. Now that we have put a name to mindsets, we can all recall a coworker with a fixed mindset. Perhaps that person was difficult or judgmental. But if that person was in a position of authority or a leader, he or she may have negatively affected the entire culture.

---

[5] Dweck video: https://www.youtube.com/watch?v=Yl9TVbAal5s.

Friend and expert on the subject of cultures of silence and cultures of voice, Rob Bogosian attested that organizations go silent for fear-based reasons, and the healthiest organizations have a culture of voice stemming from a strong perception of *psychological safety and trust*.[6] A successful ambidextrous culture has at its core a culture of safety and trust and is *never, ever, silent!*

---

[6] Bogosian, R., & Casper, C. M. (2014). *Breaking corporate silence: How high-influence leaders create cultures of voice.* https://rvbassociates.com/the-book/

3

Leadership

book that came out several years ago claimed there were over 1,500 definitions of leadership![7] With so many different interpretations out there, is there any one true definition of leadership? In ambidextrous organizations (AOs) today, various types of leadership are being discussed that allow the organization to thrive in both exploitative and explorative environments. As you discover these varying leadership types, they will reveal leaders you hadn't previously noticed.

what is this model? you buried the lead

Three Types of Leaders

The *ambidextrous leadership model* says there are three types of leaders present in the organization at any given time. *Managers* focus on current complexity in the organization, *leaders* focus on change and moving the organization to where it is going next, and *entrepreneurs* focus on opportunities. These three different positions bring different skills and abilities along with their company roles, and ambidexterity (exploitation and exploration) occurs at the intersection of these behaviors.

Complexity leadership, like the ambidextrous leadership model, is composed of three leaders. An *adaptive* leader focuses on change, an *administrative* leader focuses on current operations (think of a conductor who keeps the trains running on time for a railroad), and

---

[7] Kellerman, B. (2012). *The end of leadership.* https://www.barnesandnoble.com/w/the-end-of-leadership-barbara-kellerman/1103601419

enabling leaders focus on people and supporting their success (think of enabling leadership as kin to servant leadership[8]).

It's important to note that in an AO, all the leaders in our definitions are assumed to be equals in their respective status and potency. This is often not the case, however, in non-AO organizations with more rigid or vertical structures. For them, some of these other leadership positions may in fact be present but be informal, smaller in stature, or unacknowledged. In some unfortunate cases, the administrative leader might be the 800-pound gorilla in the room, overpowering and overshadowing the enabling and adaptive leaders. Such dominant behavior would most likely drive those leaders to take a passive back seat role or simply disappear. If you *do* work for an overpowering administrative leader, then any good done by other leaders would go unrecognized amid an overbearing train conductor with a single-minded purpose and a pocket watch. In the AO, there are a few additional models that enhance an ambidextrous leader's effectiveness.

Do either of the leadership models have to be made up of three separate individuals? Not necessarily. If you think you have the ability to assume all three positions from either model yourself, go for it. However, you may first want to look around and see if any of your people are already informally assuming these roles and maybe encourage *them* to go for it!

Two Additional Types of Leaders

The learning leader. Perhaps the most important test of an AO is the way in which it learns and executes that learning. For this reason, the ambidextrous leader must have the heart of a learner. Many savvy companies today are making room for an intriguing new position in the "C suite" known as the CLO, chief learning officer. This "chief" position gives learning an equal ranking in the leadership structure alongside performance and represents an attempt to keep learning in organizations from taking a back seat to

---

[8] Greenleaf, R. (2016). What is servant leadership? https://www.greenleaf.org/what-is-servant-leadership/

performance, since learning has a powerful, albeit indirect, link to improved performance.

The helping leader. *Adaptive, administrative,* and *enabling* are all concepts linked to positive behaviors, not the least of which is helping.[9] Ambidextrous leaders who are helpers develop a positive legacy of service for their organization and people to include growing relationships, demonstrating networking, creating goodwill, and courageously taking on new skills. A healthy helping strategy is never focused on payout or directly concerned with performance. Rather, helping done right is like a sleight-of-hand trick: shift your focus and intent from the potential pay out to the experience of being helpful and positive ancillary results magically appear.

Emotional Quotient and the Ambidextrous Leader

Emotional quotient (EQ) or emotional intelligence[10] has garnered a lot of attention for over a decade, and many companies around the world now consider EQ to be as important as, or more important than, raw intelligence quotient (IQ). Perceiving, understanding, and managing emotions effectively are all attributes of the high-EQ individual, and qualities like self-awareness, self-management, good social skills, and empathy are cornerstones of this intelligence. Possessing emotional intelligence is vital to the ambidextrous leader, and the qualities of a high-EQ person bolster their ambidextrous success. The good news about EQ is that unlike IQ, which is a *you get what you're born with* deal, emotional intelligence can be learned.

A few years ago, I conducted a study on a high-tech company on the Great Lakes. The focus was to determine whether they were ambidextrous. Not only did it turn out they were, practicing all three types of ambidexterity, but they were also doing things

---

[9] Shein, E. (2009). *Helping: How to offer, give, and receive help.* https://www.barnesand noble.com/w/helping-edgar-h-schein/1100395573

[10] Goleman, D., & Boyatzis, R. E. (2017). Emotional intelligence has 12 elements. Which do you need to work on? *Harvard Business Review.* https://hbr.org/2017/02/emotional-intelligence-has-12-elements-which-do-you-need-to-work-on

ambidextrously that the largest, most innovative companies in the world were doing. One evening after a day of conducting field research at the manufacturing facility, I sat down to dinner with the owner. I silently pondered between casual conversation how it was that this little company was practicing all three types of ambidexterity. I knew from my interview with the owner that he had a background in education (grade school teacher, I assumed) coupled with a passion since youth for anything mechanical. I got the high-tech/learning connection, but how did that dovetail with the company's consistent performance? What was the catalyst that enabled him to be an effective ambidextrous leader? As I reflected on images of him walking the factory floor in the previous days, talking with machinists, carrying equipment, taking an interest in what employees were doing, encouraging, mentoring, and helping, a thought came to my mind that I had not previously considered, and I asked, "Mike, were you ever a coach?" At that moment he stopped and looked at me in silence considering my question, and with a big smile on his face and a gleam in his eye he nodded enthusiastically, "Yes." He said in a modest voice, "and I was a pretty good one!"

The Intersection of Leadership and Culture

Before we leave culture and leadership behind us, let's make a quick stop at their intersection with Edgar Schein's elegantly simple yet powerful culture model. It's important for leaders to consider this model periodically to keep things healthy. According to Schein, organizational cultures have three components in ascending order (or each affecting the other). Any incongruencies or disparities in the different layers will ultimately manifest in friction, and it may not be immediately apparent what is happening and where the friction is coming from. These undiagnosed maladies may linger for years.

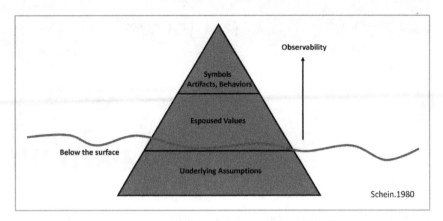

The culture model of Edgar Schein (1980).[11]

In Schein's culture model, the top of the pyramid represents the company's artifacts, symbols, and behaviors. This can be everything from the marquee on the building to the annual company picnic; these things are most seen. The next layer, espoused values, includes everything the company says and does—in documents, rules, human resource manuals, and meetings. These are the things your company wants you to know, adhere to, and believe. Last are the underlying assumptions, which are informal and usually hidden. This is what people actually do, say, believe, and tell each other. This is seen in phrases like "let me tell you how it's really done around here" and "the manual says to do it this way, but here's what everyone really does" and even "that's the rules but leadership doesn't do it." By now it should be easy to see that if your layers don't match harmoniously in Schein's culture model, if they are contradictory or hypocritical, your culture could be in rough waters, which will hurt your bottom line.

[11] Schein, E. (1980). *Organizational culture and leadership*. Fifth edition (2017): https://www.amazon.com/gp/product/1119212049/ref=dbs_a_def_rwt_bibl_vppi_i2

4

Learning

Picture this: You're standing on a street corner in a city after a rain when a car speeds by, plowing through a large puddle feet from where you're standing. Your pants are soaked through. You just learned something! Learning in organizations can feel like this at times. It can be *intentional* and *structured*, as in the case of planned training, or it can be *unintentional* and *unstructured*, as in learning where to stand on a city street after a rain. The truth is that learning happens every minute of the day and can come from anywhere. In great organizations, *all* learning is recognized, captured, shared, encouraged, and valued every bit as much as performance.

We started this book by talking about the bottom line for organizations: Organizational exploitation drives out exploration. As organizations exploit the market doing what they do best, they consequently stop exploring and learning new things. When they adopt this exploitative *lather, rinse,* and *repeat* mindset, they lose their ability to leverage new learning and perform in ways that would guarantee future success. Learning is the hub of every successful company, and this chapter discusses the ways in which learning supports the ambidextrous organization.

Organizational Learning or Learning Organization

Words matter, so pick the ones that will define your organization carefully. The names we assign our processes and behaviors affect us in subtle yet profound ways, and it's likely you are unaware of them. Take *organizational learning,* a familiar phrase synonymous with annual training and benefits briefings. Organizational learning processes do everything from correct errors and behavior to conduct required training. It's also a term which, if each word is defined individually, is an oxymoron, antithetical, and, unless you're an ambidextrous organization, practically impossible. When you consider the definition of the word "organization" you discover it denotes a "parsing down" of items to a selected chosen few, whereas "learning" suggests a widening of the aperture, considering a larger, more inclusive selection. Given these conflicting definitions, it's no wonder organizational learning is difficult to achieve at any except the smallest of incremental levels.

A *learning organization,* by contrast, does not carry the same contradictions. Learning organizations are organizations where people continually learn how to learn together and experience emergent, spontaneous learning often directed from the ground up. David Schwandt and Michael Marquardt suggested that ambidextrous companies bridge a gap from organizational learning to the learning organization.[12] They practice "learning in action," in which programmed knowledge, combined with questioning, reflection, and group learning, support performance.

Creating a Dynamic Learning Environment

If the single most important thing a CEO does for the organization is set the *culture,* then the single most important thing culture does is create and protect a *dynamic learning environment.* It's not enough to allow and encourage learning; you must protect and defend it too. What can you do to promote a dynamic (ambidextrous) learning organization? Try these ideas for starters.

1. Allow workers to behave in risky ways. Give workers freedom to explore creatively; as Teresa Amabile says, "Explore the maze." Unless you're sure your employees are about to burn the place down, leave them alone and see what happens.

---

[12] Schwandt, D., & Marquardt, M. J. (1999). *Organizational learning: From world-class theories to global best practices.* https://www.amazon.com/Organizational-Learning-David-R-Schwandt/dp/1574442597

Ref

2. Perturb learning. In their working paper "Wellsprings of creation," Brunner et al. prescribed a culture that includes intentionally "shaking things up" or "perturbing" specialized exploitative routines to break cultural inertia (becoming too rigid in thinking and practice).[13] This is a great technique for promoting new learning and exposing underperforming processes that on the surface may appear to be running efficiently. Learning inside an organization must be greater than changes outside, and an organization must learn faster than its competitors. By perturbing your own processes, you expose yourself to more learning opportunities than your competitors and experience a higher percentage of changes than would be encountered normally through routine operations. Leverage perturbation to continually renew and refresh your learning processes.

3. Make questions safe. Somewhere along the line, asking questions fell from favor, even to the point of becoming unsafe. Michael Marquardt, modern-day father of an amazing tool known as action learning,[14] would say this point happens in early adolescence when society tells children to "stop asking so many questions"—the inference being that *"questions"* are not a good thing. Mike has dedicated more than 30 years to refining this tool now used by organizations all over the world. A deceptively simple process harnessing the power of questions, action learning uses a certified coach, two ground rules, and six components to produce results that change cultures. With all the elements in place, it's like a magic card trick and works every time to solve urgent organizational problems, develop leaders, and build high-performing teams. Perhaps most remarkably, action learning creates heterogeneous learning cultures in record time—cultures set upon the highest, most inclusive, and respectful norms with no destructive storming in the process. Action learning *changes lives* and perhaps makes a

---

[13] Brunner, D. J., Staats, B. R., Tushman, M. L., & Upton, D. M. (2010). *Wellsprings of creation: How perturbation sustains exploration in mature organizations* [Working paper]. http://www.hbs. edu/faculty/Publication%20Files/09-011_157d21ea-7371-4786-8f77-ccd0943e7f98.pdf

[14] Marquardt, M. (2004). Harnessing the power of action learning. *TD, 58*(6), 26-32. https://wial.org/wp-content/uploads/Harnessing_the_Power_of_Action_Learning.pdf

critical course correction, going all the way back to our childhood. Check out the World Institute of Action Learning and consider putting this tool in your toolbox. And let me know should you need a coach—I know a guy!

Radical, revolutionary learning is considered unadvisable in most organizations and rightfully so; most would be unequipped to deal with it. Usually, only learning and innovation tethered to the familiar is culturally allowed and structurally accommodated. David Owens, author of *Creative People Must Be Stopped* (2011), described what he termed *adaptive learning* and *radical learning*, associating them with exploitation and exploration. When learning and innovation are considered together, Owens contended, "*all* but the 'smallest' incremental innovation is a bridge too far to consider adopting," though it may be precisely what is needed.

4. Find your bricoleurs, iconoclasts, polymaths, and divergent thinkers. These people are your Marvel Avengers team! What is a *bricoleur*? Think of the television character MacGyver who could get out of a locked room with nothing more than a piece of chewing gum and a paper clip. In a now-famous story, sense-making researcher Karl Weick described the Mann-Gulch disaster and backwoods firefighter Wagner Dodge.[15] Dodge and his team of fire-jumpers were racing up a steep hill of dried chaparral grass trying to escape a fire while carrying heavy packs. With strong winds and a wall of flames in close pursuit, Dodge did the unthinkable. He lit a fire in front of him and instructed his men to step into the embers of the burnt grass and lay down. A few of the men who trusted Dodge implicitly did as he said while the rest who couldn't make sense of what he was doing ran around the burnt patch continuing up the hill. Dodge had never thought of doing such a thing before; by all accounts, no one had. But he did know fire needed three things to exist: heat, a fuel source, and oxygen. By taking away one of the required elements, he broke the chain. The

---

[15] Weick, K. E. (1993). The collapse of sensemaking in organizations: The Mann Gulch disaster. *Administrative Science Quarterly*, *38*, 628-652. https://www.nifc.gov/safety/mann_gulch/suggested_reading/The_Collapse_of_Sensemaking_in_Organizations_The_Mann_Gulch.pdf

wall of flames parted around the men who followed Dodge into the burnt spot. Bricoleurs are constantly taking the things they know and recombining them in radical new ways to solve problems.

Iconoclasts are people who attack cherished beliefs or institutions; they are defined as "destroyers of images." Iconoclasts are great for exposing cultural and structural inertia, two debilitating ailments that silently cripple organizations. Set boundaries for your iconoclasts; they must be respectful and not get personal in their critique. But don't be intimidated by these positive deviants or drive them out. Passionate individuals care deeply about what they believe in, and if they believe in your company, that's a great thing. Finally, it's good to have a person in the room with a different opinion!

Polymaths, and generalists, are once again poised to have their day. A polymath is a person of wide-ranging knowledge and learning (think Leonardo da Vinci). Where once the narrowed specialist was revered as king, the master generalist is now making a comeback. In a complex changing world, creativity and diverse interests combined with expertise are being recognized as powerful tools. Most recently billionaire Mark Cuban said—and fellow billionaire Elon Musk agreed—that "freer thinkers with different perspectives are needed" and "creativity and flexible thinking should be seen as valuable assets."[16]

Divergent thinkers see the bigger picture, the whole landscape, and suspend judgment until decisions must be made. If *divergent thinkers* were to cast a net, it would be a wide one. They would be looking to catch as many species of fish as they could, while the *convergent thinker* would be busy separating the blue fish from the red ones. The workplace is full of convergent thinkers (specialists) narrowing down solutions to make quick decisions while divergent thinkers are still looking in all the corners, holding back, and asking ever more refined questions. Use your divergent thinkers strategically; keep the funnel going both ways (diverge and

---

[16] CNBC. (2018). https://www.msn.com/en-us/money/careersandeducation/mark-cuban-says-this-skill-will-be-critical-in-10-years-and-elon-musk-agrees/ar-BBL6DGN?ocid=spartandhp

converge) in cyclical patterns until you've refined the best solution for you. Interestingly, in a testament to the value of a diverse workforce, neuroscience tells us women are considerably better equipped to handle big-picture, divergent, landscape thinking.

Jackrabbits and Slow Learners

The study of organizational ambidexterity gained momentum with Duncan's theory that companies had "switching rules" and periodically switched back and forth between exploitative and explorative practices. Then James March came along in 1981, turbocharging Duncan's research with the introduction of learning. When this happened, the floodgates opened and more scholars made contributions responding to March's introduction. Evolutionary learning, revolutionary learning, radical and punctuated learning, perturbation—this is when things began to really get exciting!

I found one of March's ideas particularly intriguing, and it's something that my adult students and business and organizational professionals have also resonated with. It's the idea of fast and slow learners in the workplace, our perceptions of them, and the actual contributions they make. This idea has caused many to take account of and look more closely at what is going on under the hood within their companies.

In organizations, there are fast learners and slow learners. I call the fast learners jackrabbits. Within each organization there is an accumulated wealth of knowledge we will call the organizational code. Think of the code like a cloud of learned practices, knowledge, and behavior floating above the organization— everything the organization learns and knows is there. In the course of work, members act and interact on the playing field of business, and in the course of work they take from and contribute to this codified accumulated company knowledge.

Regarding our different learners, fast and slow, March discovered something remarkable. Of the two types, slow learners contributed more to the codified cumulative knowledge of the organization. The fast learners often contributed little to nothing by comparison while still (additionally) taking knowledge from the code. This is shocking considering that fast learners are frequently celebrated and lauded as high performers and rewarded with freer reign, autonomy, and higher pay, while slow learners or conscientious mistake makers are seen as underperforming and detrimental and are demoted, restricted, and micromanaged. Consequently, these slow learners are often made negative examples of, persecuted, and pushed out of the company when their learning contributions are the greatest. Such actions can send powerfully troubling messages regarding learning, sharing, contributing, and communication.

Akin to ideas in Daniel Kahneman's book *Thinking Fast and Slow*, in which he says we naturally think in two ways (fast or slow), both types of learners and thinkers are required in organizations for healthy, sustainable performance and growth, and we must understand the value of each.

5

Structure

Structure in an ambidextrous organization (AO) is at times vertical and hierarchical, and at other times horizontal, dependent upon internal as well as external factors. The ability to change structural postures when needed, however, is difficult if not impossible for most organizations.

Structural Alignment

Allan Afuah provided insights into ambidexterity in his study of incremental and discontinuous technological change.[17] If a structural path into an old technology was vertical, he contended, then the organization would perform poorly in integrating a new technology. If the organization was not aligned vertically into the old technology, however, the organization would perform well in integrating the new technology. The implications for learning strategies in this study suggest that firms need to have both vertical and horizontal structures at their disposal and be capable of navigating and pursuing evolutionary as well as revolutionary changes using different learning.

What is a vertical structural path into a technology versus a horizontal one (or none at all)? A vertical structure is one that is refined, established, and mechanized. In other words, it has been around in your organization for a while, with all the bugs and kinks

---

[17] Afuah, A. (2018). *Business model innovation.* https://www.amazon.com/Business-Model-Innovation-Concepts-Analysis/dp/1138330523/ref=sr_1_1?hvadid=78477695887288&hvbmt=bp&hvdev=c&hvqmt=p&keywords=allan+afuah&qid=1563290261&s=gateway&sr=8-1

smoothed out. It's likely a money-making lather, rinse, and repeat process set in motion some time ago.

Evolutionary changes come upon organizations slowly over time, while revolutionary changes are punctuated, sudden, and even shocking to an organization's systems. This also says something significant about structural inertia, a phenomenon wherein an organization can become so rigid in its structural processes, vertical or horizontal, that it can no longer flex, bend, or accommodate anything new, including market changes and opportunities, and it can suffer.

The solution? Have both vertical and horizontal structural processes and models that you can call upon when needed. Whether this means leadership, management, workforce, or activity processes, you get the idea. Whatever you discover, go after, or encounter, you have a template you can quickly apply. As discussed, many organizations discard or discourage their most explorative, creative, and innovative people once the company shifts into "exploitation mode," deeming them no longer useful. However, when an existing paradigm shifts, everyone and every-thing engaged in the status quo goes back to zero. When this happens, those companies could certainly use those forward, out-of-the-box independent thinkers they once had.

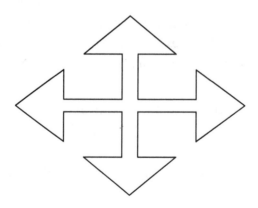

Structural Obstacles to Radical Learning

The tyranny of now is always biting at an organization's heels. It can have the effect of keeping the collective anxiety of the organization high enough to promote almost exclusive exploitative activity and subsequently only exploitative learning. It would be fair to say that exploitation is sometimes the enemy of exploration and break-through learning. In his video *The Divided Brain*,[18] Ian McGilchrist suggested that structural decisions come down to an argument between the hemispheres of the brain. The argument of the left hemisphere (more closely associated with exploitative thinking) is a more convincing one than the argument of the right because it shaves off everything from its model which it does not like and everything which is not already known; there are no risky "what if's" in the left hemisphere's thinking.

Restructuring Structure

To begin to rejig your current structure for increased performance and stability, you need go no further than to relax your stance and thoughtfully consider where your organization and its members appear to be going and what they are doing. If your organization seems preoccupied with marching ahead with arbitrary internal processes, bogged down in bureaucracy and complicated rules and activities that are outdated or nonsensical, then you could be suffering from structural inertia. When this happens, organizations become too rigid and inflexible to explore desired strategies or to prepare to exploit the next big thing when it is spotted on the horizon.

If the single most important thing a CEO does for the organization is setting the *culture*, then the single most important thing culture does is create a flexible organizational structure and play field in which its members are as equally comfortable running with scissors as they are building a jigsaw puzzle. It's not enough to learn to do something well and then do it to exhaustion; you also

---

[18] https://www.youtube.com/watch?v=dFs9WO2B8uI

have to stretch yourself, stay on the steep side of the learning curve, and be ready to change structurally. What can you do to promote a dynamic (ambidextrous) learning organization with the structural flexibility to pivot and change? Consider these ideas for starters.

1. Have a chief learning officer (CLO). When we are too close to a perceived threat in our path, often we bite without thinking. This in turn can encourage a *pack mentality* of like-mindedness as mirror neurons in the brain naturally cause us to empathetically mimic the behavior of others. Before long, everyone is biting and getting bitten. This is one of the things that happens when performance is the only voice allowed at the leadership table, and it illustrates the association between performance, exploitation, and exploitative learning. Mainly exploitation is too reflexive, narrowly focused, and scripted to be the sole source of learning and experience for an organization. Exploitation is more performance based, and exploration is more innovation based. Additionally, companies that perceive everything in terms of performance and exploitation require only their best performers to take care of the critical things and use only traditional solutions (like biting); they don't learn anything new or give new people opportunities to learn.

Many companies are remedying this dilemma by making room at the table for a new position known as the chief learning officer, or CLO. This position gives learning equal ranking in the organization alongside performance and represents a desire to keep learning from taking a back seat to performance. CLOs are a champion for learning and know the difference between exploitative learning and explorative learning—and the need for both within the organization. They can interpret complex dynamics of social interaction and help members and leaders alike understand the why behind the what, enriching understanding and bolstering motivation and buy in for performance and learning to be present and move together. Furthermore, CLOs encourage organizations to slow down and resist gut feelings. Think of the CLO as your personal learning coach on the sidelines.

2. Examine the field of play. *Field theory, structuration,* and *habitus* may be alien concepts and sound completely foreign, but they represent the simple idea that organizations and social groups are similar to soccer or football games. The model below, compiled from the works of Anthony Giddens, Kurt Lewin, Pierre Bourdieu, and Edgar Schein, illustrates how organizations and individuals interact to change one another. The concept goes like this: As agents (organizational members) enter a field of play (the organization), they interact with other players on the field. During their activities, they act out scripts (behavioral patterns)—written partially by the organization, partially by their interactions with others, and partially by themselves—and they affect and are affected by these exchanges on the field of play. This ultimately becomes part of an action realm of organizational activity (depicted at the bottom of the model). At the same time, they are also receiving from and contributing to an institutional realm of codified knowledge accumulated by the organization (depicted at the top of the model). This institutional realm can be thought of as a *cloud* of knowledge collected by the organization in the form of norms, data, practices, stories, beliefs, etc.

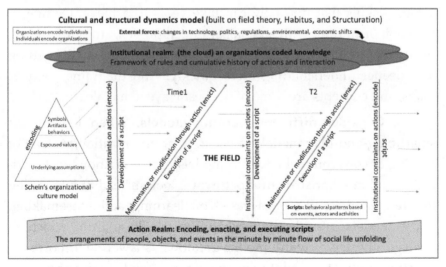

Cultural and structural dynamics model (Zabiegalski, 2018).

Why is this important to know and consider? First, it's significant because this ongoing exchange says something crucial about structure and learning: namely, that agents, their institutions, and the play field act as stressors and influencers upon one another, either challenging and modifying or supporting and reinforcing the current organizational structure. They're complex, unpredictable, and not entirely known until it's all over. Proof of this can be found in the idea that as these agents contribute to the accumulated codified knowledge of the organization and interact with others on the field while executing scripts, this execution of scripts does not always involve awareness or intentionality; actors may simply behave according to their perception of the way things are. The ultimate enactment of a script will be partially known and partially unknown by us on the field and not "completely" known until it has played out.

Second, studying diagrams like these promotes something called *metalearning*. Simply put, metalearning means learning how to learn. Diagrams, concepts, maps, and models give us a big-picture understanding. Metalearning helps us learn how to look for the big picture; it's a way to set a structure or plan for learning and subsequently build strategies and achieve deep knowledge of a subject—skills that normally can take years to achieve. Getting in the habit of starting with a metalearning approach, studying the big picture before rushing onto the field, is a better strategy for getting to a deeper understanding more quickly. And diagrams, models, maps, and concepts are some of the best ways to metalearn.

3. Consider different learning models. When looking for smart plug-and-play models to use in your organization, instead of looking at conventional decision models based on known categorization and familiar structural pathways, look instead at integrating different models, like ones based on learning and sensemaking. These models provide a more appropriate base from which to strategically step forward into the unknown, answering tomorrow's questions rather than reinforcing what you already know and do.

One such model is the Cynefin (pronounced CAN-AV-IN) framework created by Welsh researcher Dave Snowden.[19] What's unique about this model is that, unlike other models based upon traditional categorization with a four-quadrant framework applying known best practices, the Cynefin is a complexity, sensemaking decision model. In this model, *data* precede the framework (not the other way around), making it perfect for AOs. In Snowden's model, the decision *patterns* or *frameworks* emerge from the data, revealing new and more productive patterns (frameworks). Traditional categorization decision models are good for informing *exploitation* practices because they take what is already known and produced and sort it in existing frameworks, but they are ill advised to tackle *exploration* strategies and reveal new strengths and emerging practices. What's different about Snowden's model is that it is perfect for the AO engaging in explorative, innovative, or creative behavior.

4. Perturb learning. Perturbing learning was discussed as a strategy for creating a learning environment but applies to structure as well. Intentionally "shaking things up" or "perturbing" specialized exploitative routines to break cultural or structural inertia[20] is a great technique for keeping your structure from becoming too rigid to change when it wants or needs to. By perturbing your own processes, you expose yourself to greater learning opportunities and experience a higher percentage of changes than would be encountered normally through routine operations. Think of this as

---

[19] See YouTube video: https://www.youtube.com/watch?time_continue=3&v=N7oz366X0-8.
Giddens, A. (1984). *The constitution of society: Outline of the theory of structuration.* http://www.urbanlab.org/articles/anthropology/Giddens%201984%20-%20The%20 Constitution%20of%20Society.pdf
Bourdieu, P. (1977). *Outline of a theory of practice.* https://www.cambridge.org/core/books/ outline-of-a-theory-of-practice/193A11572779B478F5BAA3E3028827D8
Lewin, K. (1951). *Field theory in social science.* https://www.amazon.com/Field-Theory-Social-Science-Theoretical/dp/B000JJ0WN2
Schein, E. (1980). *Organizational culture and leadership.* Fifth edition (2017): https://www. amazon.com/gp/product/1119212049/ref=dbs_a_def_rwt_bibl_vppi_i2
Barley, S. R., & Tolbert, P. S. (1997). Institutionalization and structuration: Studying the links between action and institution. *Organization Studies, 18,* 93-117.
[20] Brunner, D. J., Staats, B. R., Tushman, M. L., & Upton, D. M. (2010). *Wellsprings of creation: How perturbation sustains exploration in mature organizations* [Working paper]. http://www.hbs. edu/faculty/Publication%20Files/09-011_157d21ea-7371-4786-8f77-ccd0943e7f98.pdf

a routine structural earthquake drill. Leverage perturbation to continually refresh learning processes and shake your structural foundations to see how strong and flexible they really are!

The Ambidextrous Ecosystem

A review of structure in an AO wouldn't be complete without a discussion of the ambidextrous ecosystem. The ecosystem model is a conglomeration of ideas to depict what I call the ambidextrous ecosystem broken down into culture, learning, and social learning cycles. In the ecosystem, people move through different environments, phases, and experiences in the course of their work. They behave exploitatively and exploratively; they encounter and use uncodified and codified knowledge, tacit knowledge (only in one person's head), and explicit knowledge (shared and known by everyone); and they learn, share, and collaborate.[21]

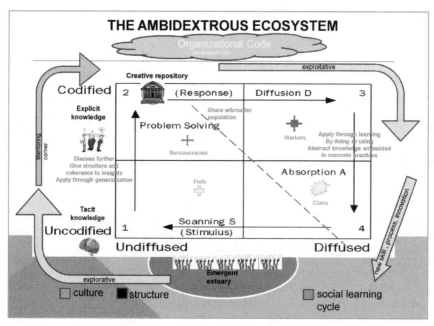

The ambidextrous ecosystem (Zabiegalski, 2015).

[21] Boisot, M., Nordberg, M., Yami, S., & Nicquevert, B. (2011). *Collisions and collaborations.* https://www.amazon.com/Collisions-Collaboration-Organization-Learning-Experiment/dp/0199567921

Two areas I have added worthy of note are the emergent estuary at the bottom and the creative repository in the upper left corner. All true AOs have these areas within their organizations where members can create and nurture new ideas and then collect them for immediate use, use them later, or combine them with other ideas when the time is right. As Woody Powell said, *the hallways of most organizations are littered with the debris of alternate success*. This is not the case in AOs; there, ideas would be collected, considered, periodically reviewed, and handled respectfully, and the intern in the mailroom may have the company's next big idea.

PART II:
COMPLEXITY

6

The Science of Complexity

lbert Einstein once said, "Everything in life should be as simple as possible, but no simpler." What Einstein was alluding to was finding a formula for successful navigation in a complex universe, but not one that was too simple. In this complicated world we live in, we're constantly streamlining, simplifying, and hopefully making functional sense of the complexity that surrounds us. But has the pendulum swung too far? In creating a simplified version of reality to cope and ignoring the intricacies of life, have we ultimately paid the price of never knowing higher levels of sustained success and performance? Are we deferring our success by forgetting that life really is complicated?

This part of the book addresses organizational ambidexterity as a form of complexity and explains why it's important to move through life with a questioning mind. Today's most innovative, healthy, and successful companies don't ignore or avoid complexity; rather, they embrace it, leverage it, and study its lessons.

Complexity Science

Today's innovative companies are learning the language of complexity. There are several interchangeable concepts in organizational science that advocate paying attention to the complexities of life and business: *organizational complexity,*

complexity science, and *complex adaptive systems.* A complex adaptive system in biology is a "complex macroscopic collection" of "similar and partially connected micro-structures" formed in order to adapt to a changing environment.[22] A complex adaptive system is also a system in which a perfect understanding of the individual parts does not automatically convey an understanding of the whole.

It's helpful to note that systems can be *complex* without being *adaptive*—the difference being the system's ability to evolve or change when needed. Systems can be *complex* in that they are *dynamic networks of interactions,* and their relationships are not aggregations of the individual static entities. They can also be *adaptive* if the individual and collective behavior mutates and self-organizes according to the change-initiating micro events or collections of events. Systems are a complex macroscopic collection of similar and partially connected microstructures formed to adapt to a changing environment and increase their survivability as a macro structure. The study of complex adaptive systems in organizations blends insights from the natural and social sciences to develop system-level models and insights.

Like James March's article on exploration, exploitation, and learning,[23] Ricardo Pascale's research principles also cover learning but within the context of complex adaptive systems. A culture of ambidextrous complexity can be better understood by a recounting of the origins of Pascale's complexity science, which has been characterized as "the science of all sciences."

Origins of Complexity Theory

In his 1999 article,[24] Pascale outlined how work on organizational complexity began in the 1980s at New Mexico's Santa Fe Institute when a group of distinguished scientists with backgrounds encompassing disciplines as diverse as physics,

---

[22] https://en.wikipedia.org/wiki/Complex_adaptive_system
[23] March, J. (1991). Exploration and exploitation in organizational learning. *Organization Science, 2,* 71-87. http://www.jstor.org/stable/2634940.
[24] Pascale, R. T. (1999). Surfing the edge of chaos. *MITSloan Management Review.* https://sloanreview.mit.edu/article/surfing-the-edge-of-chaos/

microbiology, zoology, botany, paleontology, astrophysics, archeology, and economics were drawn together for one specific reason. All their disciplines shared the commonality of being made up of building blocks composed of many smaller agents that continually organized and reorganized themselves (sometimes in clashing ways) in a boundary between rigidity and randomness. These researchers wanted to know what these agents and their behaviors shared with their own disciplines.

Lessons from Physics

Newtonian physics is defined with *cause and effect, predictability,* and *certainty;* it is a world of *distinct wholes* and their parts. A reality drawn from this language is that of the observable world, *quantifiable determinism, linear thinking,* and a controllable slow-moving future with expected outcomes. Here, *mechanistic reductionist thinking* drives the day.

Quantum physics was a new way to interpret the world. Scientific theories propagated by Planck, Einstein, Bohr, and others in the early 1900s largely revised Newton's theory with its classical mechanics viewpoint and can give us a more refined picture of reality. The world of quantum physics is different in part because it is rich in relationships and is considered at a "subatomic" level. It is a world of *discrete events, emergence, complexity, fractals,* and *relationships between objects.* Not simply concerning itself with deterministic outcomes, predictability, and repetition, quantum physics also considers other phenomena such as *chaos theory* and deals with *order* and *change, autonomy* and *control, structure* and *flexibility,* and the *butterfly effect*—the idea that a small change in one area can have a large impact in another.

Because the business world of today is different from that of 250 years ago, it's time for a new operating language—one that will better characterize and frame what we encounter in the workplace and more closely support what we set out to accomplish. To the human mind, words create and define the world around us. As dramatically profound as sight, words are used to language reality into existence. Our mind uses words to not just create meaning but also operationalize behavior, navigate, and act; it is in this way that thoughts become things.

Lessons from Biology

Stanford University biologist Robert Sapolsky in a now famous lecture on emergence and complexity[25] discussed how small differences in nature can have consequences that magnify, resulting in the *butterfly effect, convergence,* and *fractals*. Illustrating this using the example of cellular automata that establish simple "local neighbor rules" for generational growth, Sapolsky discussed the few rules that can be drawn from these patterns. Of the most compelling rules governing cells, Sapolsky told us that by "looking at the mature state you cannot tell what the starting state originally was" and examining a cellular pattern starting state gives you "no indication as to what the mature state will look like." While most cellular automata patterns ultimately go extinct, Sapolsky noted one rule that does appear to ensure health, saying that introducing *asymmetry* to a starting state results in living dynamic patterns while introducing *symmetry* will not.

The implications for organizations seem to suggest that asymmetric (diverse), "not the same" patterns may have a better chance at achieving growth success, and examining a successful "mature" or "starting" state is no reliable indicator as to what it *was* or *is* going to be. This also suggests something profound for businesses regarding judgments, biases, and assumptions.

Lessons from Neuroscience

The world of the human mind is the world of the left and right hemisphere of the brain and rational and intuitive thought. Ian McGilchrist in his book *The Master and His Emissary,* outlined in the video *The Divided Brain,*[26] indicated that "thinking in the left

[25] https://www.youtube.com/watch?v=o_ZuWbX-CyE
[26] https://www.youtube.com/watch?v=dFs9WO2B8uI

hemisphere gives us *narrow, sharply focused attention to detail.*" When we already know something is important and we want to be precise, we use our left hemispheres to pin it down and manipulate it. The left hemisphere prefers things that are "*known, fixed, static, decontextualized, isolated, explicit,* generalized in nature, and ultimately lifeless," while the world of the right hemisphere gives us "*sustained, broad, alertness* and prefers things which are *open, individual, changing, evolving, interconnected,* and *implicit,* but never fully graspable or known." We combine the hemispheres in different ways to have a broad understanding of the world and at the same time manipulate it. The problem, according to McGilchrist, lies in the nature of these two worlds and their sometimes conflicted ways of thinking, as it's important to have both knowledge of the parts and the wisdom of the whole.

In the business world, people have cognitive hemispheric preferences, preferred "homerooms" of thought, and have neurological and behavior skill and experience navigating in the world of either the left or right hemisphere. The implications for exploitative and explorative (ambidextrous) behavior are obvious.

Lessons for Ambidexterity and Complexity

Recognizing a culture of ambidexterity (a culture with exploitative and explorative behavior) is important and akin to acknowledging a culture of complexity. It involves recognizing such things as *equilibrium* (balance) and *imbalance, tension, chaos,* and *emergence* as well as traditional creation and *divergent* and *convergent* thinking. In these systems, *entropy* and *negative entropy, exploitation, exploration, the butterfly effect, weak linkages,* and *fractals* could be influencers. It involves seeing *heterogeneity* and *homogeneity, incremental* and *radical* innovation, and *evolutionary* as well as *revolutionary* change. An understanding and validation of complexity by leaders and managers is of the utmost importance to help breathe an ambidextrous culture to life!

We create and change our realities every moment as we walk into and through experiences. Because of this, how we behave and are observed behaving in a complex world can make all the difference; these are the final determinants of reality. The study of complex adaptive systems in organizations blends insights from the natural and social sciences to develop system-level models and insights, allowing for new discussions of such things as emergent behavior and other intricacies frequently overlooked. Suddenly things like weak linkages between agents and the language of quantum physics become more relatable and significant.

7

Equilibrium, Symmetry, Structure, and Emergence

The last chapter introduced the concept of complexity and described how a focus on intricate processes working behind the scenes provides powerful insights that could potentially catapult your company's performance and sustainability. This chapter continues the discussion on organizational complexity and ambidexterity by unpacking the complexity concepts of *equilibrium, symmetry, structure,* and *emergence* and how they can be considered in everyday organizational practice. It's important to note the concepts and theories presented here are not absolutes; they are open to new interpretation and are meant to stimulate thought, questions, and further exploration and discussion.

Where theory meets practice is the place where the rubber meets the road, and it's the place that matters most in business. This is the place where battles are won or lost, where relationships between things are cultivated and grown or discarded and plowed under. In this place we either stretch ourselves to new understanding or fall back into the groove of the familiar and comfortable. An ambidextrous organization (AO) is, first and foremost, a learning organization, so regardless of outcomes, AOs and their members always learn and incorporate that new learning into current practice.

Equilibrium and Imbalance

Pascale outlined the ebb and flow of complex components and discussed equilibrium as organizational death, citing *entropy*—the tendency of living systems to run down, consume resources, and pursue a static state—and *negative entropy*—the renewal of systems by the introduction of new resources—as natural ways in which organizations (like living systems) breathe.[27] These systems share strong characteristics with ambidexterity due to an AO's dichotomous nature (exploitation and exploration) and emergent, diverse, and disparate properties. In other words, a closed organizational system is unsustainable over time, consuming all its resources, and very few closed systems occur in nature. One example of negative entropy (an open system) acting upon and renewing an organization is the introduction of new information and learning in business. An organization amid learning is in motion and changing structurally, behaviorally, and culturally. Organizations facing the tensions between exploitation and exploration would be in this situation of negative entropy, breathing in and out like a living system.

Symmetry, Asymmetry, and Structure

Symmetry: Pebbles in a stream. The human mind loves symmetry; it "keys in" on it, notices it, finds it aesthetically attractive, and subsequently looks for and imagines it everywhere. However, it is asymmetry that is prevalent in nature and gives us our most dynamic structures and robust systems, and often the more asymmetric and chaotic the structure, the more robust it is. Even pebbles in a stream that may first appear identical and perfectly symmetrical are not under close examination; symmetry in nature is always approximate, not exact. Biologist Robert Sapolsky, researcher Bill McKelvey, and others discussed such complexity topics as *symmetry* and a*symmetry*, *emergence* and *complexity*, and *fractals*, *chaos*, and *weak linkages*.

---

[27] Pascale, R. T. (1999). Surfing the edge of chaos. *MITSloan Management Review*. https://sloanreview.mit.edu/article/surfing-the-edge-of-chaos/

I once attended a presentation in which Bill McKelvey, professor of complexity science at UCLA,[28] presented a look at symmetry and structures. The pictures in his presentation spoke volumes. His pictures depicting structures suggested something profound—that symmetry (when it appeared to occur) came from asymmetry. Furthermore, symmetry and asymmetry (or more symmetrical and less symmetrical patterns) can develop quite different structures, such as creek beds and sand dunes as an example. As biologist Robert Sapolsky suggested in a discussion of cellular patterns and their starting and end states, you cannot tell with certainty what a mature cellular pattern will look like by studying its starting state or conversely tell what a starting state looked like by examining its mature state.[29] What Sapolsky was saying that McKelvey strikingly illustrated speaks poignantly about structures' first appearances and judgments.

Asymmetry: Dunes in the desert. When we think of asymmetry, we think of things that are uneven, unalike, not identical, or out of proportion, and we don't normally think of structures. A truth in nature is that asymmetry creates and supports structures, very dynamic strong and robust ones like the sand dune made of individual unique parts.

---

[28] https://www.anderson.ucla.edu/knowledge-assets/bill-mckelvey
[29] https://www.youtube.com/watch?v=o_ZuWbX-CyE

The building of structure: Grains of sand magnified 150 times. The implications for building strong structures in organizations are clear, whether it is pebbles in a creek or magnified grains of sand from a dune. The individual parts that contribute to the whole can be quite unique, diverse, and unalike. Diverse agents and building blocks build robust structures, and chaotic (asymmetric) structures and systems are perhaps the most robust of all.

San Diego State University mechanical engineering professor, mentor, and longtime friend George Mansfield recently shared a story with me of a late polymath friend of his who offered the following insight. He said that in nature the most chaotic structures tended to be the most robust and, comparatively, companies with more open architectures appear to have very similar kinds of chaotic structures. In his current work volunteering for innovative engineering start-ups and ad lib engineering clubs, George said the "gang-style" working meetings of these clubs appear very chaotic from the outside but produce an amazing amount of innovative interaction!

Emergent and Nonemergent Systems

"The hallways of most organizations are littered with the debris of alternate successes." —Woody Powell

We won't talk much about nonemergent systems because frankly there isn't much going on. Traditional processes from expected places are the order of the day, and in this world things don't just "bubble up." Most organizations are outrageously rich with emergent ideas, and unfortunately in most of them, these ideas are never recognized, never validated, and never realized. Why? There are different reasons, as we will discuss, but Kevin Ashton said, "Sometimes creativity threatens the stability of the status quo, and therefore creative people are stifled either by design or accident."[30]

What is emergence? In biology, philosophy, and systems theory, emergence is quite literally the appearance of something from nothing! In reality, however, it is the creation of something new from disparate smaller parts that self-organize or are pulled together to create something new that suddenly appears. It can be thought of as the bubbling up of something more complex from simpler parts. In organizations, this means the creation or appearance of new ideas, processes, or products from unexpected or unplanned places, like the janitor sweeping the shop floor who has the company's next billion-dollar idea.

Recently at a business function, I suggested my company adopt an "intrapreneurship" small business model. The idea as I envisioned it would be simple: an entrepreneurship innovation model, only internal to the organization. The company would provide a small amount of seed money and would shelter and protect the employee start-up under its umbrella with small resource contributions or support during its infancy and would share in the profits should the new venture spark and catch fire. Such a model, as I saw it, would go a long way in building a stronger organizational culture for the company, putting its money where its mouth is by showing its members it cares about what they care about. Adopting a model like this would also help the organization diversify its portfolio. Should the company's primary market begin to dry up, being diversified in other areas would make the company more drought resistant in tough economic

[30] Ashton, K. (2015). *How to fly a horse: The secret history of creation, invention, and discovery.* https://www.amazon.com/How-Fly-Horse-Invention-Discovery/dp/0804170061

times, as happened several years ago when something called sequestration created devastating budget cuts in the market. Despite knowing of at least a dozen company employees who work passionately in their spare time on their own small businesses, my idea has generated little attention or interest.

What are the chief reasons emergent ideas are frequently ignored, overlooked, or fail to take root in organizations? First, they often come from unrecognized or unendorsed areas. Because emergent ideas can come from any level in an organization or from disparate places, they are often not recognized as legitimate or worthwhile. Second, as Ashton suggested, they can come from a direction that might upset the hierarchical power or control bases and stress the structural inertia of the organization and therefore bring too much threatening baggage. Lastly, they can be heralded as too risky in terms of cost, time, or other resources to be worthwhile.

Organizations, like living systems, naturally wind down unless they refresh themselves with new energy. But for organizations, knowing when, how, and why to refresh themselves often seems to be a point of paralysis. Organizations are dissipative structures maintained by members contributing energy as they ebb and flow between a state of entropy and negative entropy, effectively breathing in and out. Learning to leverage emergence and the language of quantum physics is a vital part of creating learning networks, and it is something an ambidextrous organization intuitively knows how to do and do well.

What is the right recipe of behaviors to leverage concepts like emergence, and what ingredients would create and promote an emergent-rich environment? For organizations to thrive, they must learn to become ambidextrous, and in order to do this they must embrace newer scientific principles like quantum mechanics as their operating language and embrace the power of emergence.

8

Chaos and Governors

In scientific terms, some systems in nature are defined as *complex*, while others are also *adaptive,* but not all systems are both *complex* and *adaptive systems* (CAS). This is the place you and your organization want to be. The distinctive difference with complex adaptive systems is that unlike nonadaptive systems, they code their internal environments into many *schemata* (individual operating patterns, structures, and frameworks), and these frameworks naturally compete with one another internally. Considering the ambidextrous organization (AO) as a CAS with its exploitative and explorative behavior, it's easy to see how competing schemata would naturally reside among the exploitative and explorative components within an AO, competing for precious resources, execution, and prominence. In the AO, specific behaviors allow the tensions of these competing schemata to coexist and regulate in a self-balancing and continually changing dance. This chapter addresses that chaos and some strategies to manage it.

Chaos

While working on this chapter, I had a serendipitous discussion with a very smart software engineer friend named Ned at a company luncheon. I was explaining ambidextrous organizational structures to Ned when he brought up the subject of chaos and chaos theory. Chaos theory is a concept used in disciplines such as mathematics, economics, sociology, and philosophy to describe the occasional disorder, randomness, and unpredictability of behavior in otherwise predictable deterministic systems. As I listened to Ned talk about chaos theory and asked clarifying questions, I looked around excitedly for a white board and markers to capture the thoughts our dialogue was producing. Not finding any, I grabbed the nearest paper napkin and pen and created the *ambidextrous chaos* model.

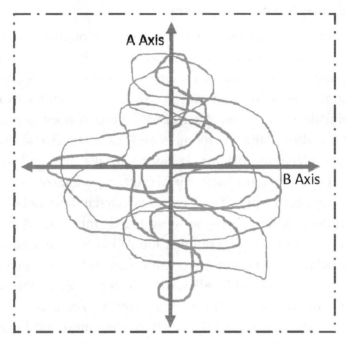

The ambidextrous chaos model (Zabiegalski, 2018).

The chaos model is designed to depict the disorder and randomness (chaos) that inevitably occur in organizations, defined as any new or unexpected behaviors or processes outside of expected or prescribed norms. Axis A of this model represents a vertical structure and norms which might be present within an organization, while Axis B represents a horizontal structure. It's important to note that the depiction of this model is predicated upon the organization having both a vertical business structure (as in a military unit, for example) and a horizontal structure, as in an innovative tech start-up. The idea that AOs contain both vertical and horizontal structural pathways in leadership, management, processes, and behaviors, as this model depicts, illustrates this AO mindset and gives it the unique ability to pivot in both exploitative and explorative ways as the environment changes. The ability to meet and support rapid transition with a shift from one structure (axis) to the other to mirror environmental market changes with corresponding behavioral changes gives AOs a distinct advantage over less adaptive non-AO systems.

In science, *chaos theory* says that even though some systems may be considered deterministic, meaning their future behavior is determined by their initial conditions, this is true only as long as no random elements are introduced. To put it another way, the deterministic nature of a deterministic system does not make it predictable due to the randomness and disorder (chaos) that may inevitably creep in, driving behavior to the left and right of predicted outcomes in a hierarchical (vertical) organizational model or above and below predicted outcomes in a flat (horizontal) model. Furthermore, when chaos is introduced into the AO model (represented by the squiggly line), the AO is at a clear advantage. Chaotic behavior in this environment is seen as less threatening and can be more comfortably allowed to emerge. Even though this behavior might stray from one or the other axis, it is still identifiable as potentially productive, as it can be found and interpreted in relation to the other axis—as moving away from one axis moves it towards the other. It is now bound somewhere within the borders of one of the two axes (depicted by the dotted line) in a grid-like pattern. Chaos allowed to ensue within framed borders in this manner is invaluable to the AO and represents the source of its learning power, providing new insights, revolutionary learning opportunities, innovation, and ultimately higher performance and productivity than other nonadaptive organizational systems. Because of the AO's reinforced dual structure, emergent chaos is made better sense of, is more easily harnessed, and appears less threatening and more positively interpreted. Whether or not chaos can be completely controlled is a matter for debate; however, such a model helps chaos to be welcomed and controlled enough to be productive within the edges of the imaginary boundary drawn around the axis.

In this way, AOs are superior at managing processes to interpret, support, and potentially leverage unpredicted behavior that strays from current or acceptable norms. Chaos tolerated in this fashion also provides strong reinforcing value in the form of innovation, new learning, and culture. Here's a foot-stomper for organizations: In physics and biology, systems are optimally efficient and robust when they can maintain themselves at the edge of chaos. The important question for organizations is clear: When should behaviors or processes be managed at the edge of chaos, and perhaps more importantly, how do we manage the fear of possibly flying too close to the sun and losing control?

Managing at the Edge of Chaos: A Cautionary Tale Half Told

These days, it seems as if organizations have taken the Greek myth of Icarus to heart, but they only have half the story. As the legend goes, Daedalus made a pair of wings for his son Icarus to use to escape prison. Before he gave his son the wings, however, Daedalus offered a warning: Don't fly too close to the sun or the wax holding the wings together will melt. Icarus, ignoring his father's warning, flew too close to the sun anyway, and sure enough his wings disintegrated, plummeting him to his death. This cautionary tale we've heard so many times warns us against taking risks, reaching too far or too high. What's curiously missing from this story is that this was only half of Daedalus' warning. Daedalus also told his son not to fly too low; doing so, he said, would cause the spray from the sea to saturate his wings, also dragging him to his death. Why do organizations try to eliminate risk and put constraining governors on their employees? Given the chance, would employees behave as cautiously as their leaders or go for the sun?

When I was a kid, I spent many a summer evening at my favorite go-cart track with my friends. While at the track, one of us, sometimes more than one, would invariably come equipped with a flat-headed (slotted) screwdriver in their back pocket. On the go-carts engine there was a mechanical device called a governor and on the governor was a slotted screw. We learned early on that by either backing the screw out with a screwdriver or tightening it down, you could decrease, or increase, the speed of the engine, adjusting peak performance and speed on the go-cart. We knew the go-cart track owner had "de-tuned" all of the engines before we ran out to jump behind the wheel and the minute his back was turned one of us ran from cart to cart asking the other racers if they wanted us to "tune up" their engine for them. What I remember most about those experiences was that no kid, *ever*, refused an offer to make the engine go faster, much less ask to have it made to go slower.

Governors can come from many places; the brain is a natural governor for the body, as our mind mentally sets our body's physical limits. As Maxwell Maltz noted, however, it's rare for people to actually "use up" all their physical energy; our bodies can muster much more endurance than we think.[31] Governors can also be imposed by others and therefore sometimes feel real. I don't know if governors in organizations filter down from leadership or are dispensed by fellow employees and an established culture, or perhaps both. And I'm not sure of the reasons why. Do we wish to protect each other, protect ourselves, or keep others from surpassing us on the track? Whatever the reason, we need to be aware and careful of our actions. Educator Fred Rogers once said, "The worst thing a person can do to another is diminish them." I believe this and would further add that our only job in life should be to encourage one another daily to stay away from the ground and reach for the sun!

---

[31] Maltz, M. (2015). *Psycho-cybernetics*. https://www.amazon.com/Psycho-Cybernetics-Updated-Expanded-Maxwell-Maltz/dp/0399176136

PART III:
THE AMBIDEXTROUS MIND

9

Cultivating the Ambidextrous Mind

Earlier chapters discussed complexity, adaptation, getting comfortable with chaos, and focusing on one another with support and courage. In this part of the book, I continue to use quantum mechanics as a template and shift the focus from the "outer" space of organizational activities to the "inner" space of the individual mind navigating the outer organization space. This is the beginning of an argument in defense of the intuitive (explorative) mind as an active important co-author in the rational (exploitative) mind, an argument long made by many classical and contemporary scientists. It's also an appeal to get your "mental house" in order, stave off judgment, and prepare you to think in new (more considerate) ways. You cannot truly master the rational side of your mind without also addressing the intuitive.

I have a humble goal: by the end of this book you will think ambidextrously, shift easily from exploitative to explorative mindsets, dwell in either place with concentration and comfort, and be in better command of your inner mind as you bring it to bear upon the outer world. As intuitive thinker Bob Proctor[32] noted, *"Most of us have it dead wrong. We let the outside world control the inside when really it should be the other way around."*

---

[32] https://www.proctorgallagherinstitute.com/workshops

While finishing the last chapter of this book, I had a watershed moment, perhaps a watershed week. In that short span of time, I perfectly coalesced the thoughts of a previous article, I discovered a Seminole book written in 1975 which succinctly defined my views concerning the link between organizational complexity and quantum theory, and I escaped to a movie with my wife which quite unexpectedly illustrated my current writing so poignantly it caused me to laugh out loud in the theatre, shaking the feeling it was a personal message meant just for me. True to the definition, the turning-point events of that week created a mental dividing line, a watershed, which seemed to "synchronize" the events of my life.

> "The intuitive mind is a sacred gift and the rational mind is a faithful servant. We have created a society that has honored the servant but forgotten the gift." –Albert Einstein

Cultivating the ambidextrous mind and giving allegiance to both the servant and the gift as Einstein said is not just a societal nicety; not doing so would be downright blasphemy. We are intuitively and rationally built to think equally in explorative and exploitative ways. The problem comes as we are encouraged and trained in our professional and social lives from an early age to only behave in one of these ways, woefully neglecting or even denying the other. This creates an imbalance that torments our organizations and personal lives needlessly. Late mindfulness guru and self-help author Wayne Dyer[33]—who said *"when you change the way you look at things, the things you look at change"*—learned to master this balance and navigate between these two realms effortlessly. Dyer also spoke about watershed events and synchronicity in his life, in which he would be searching for a passage to cite for a forthcoming project when a book would fall from a shelf at his feet with the very idea he was searching for, someone would engage him in random conversation and it would answer the current question on his mind,

---

[33] https://www.drwaynedyer.com/

or he would unexpectedly walk into an experience that would bring him the answer he was searching for.

In my humble opinion, if are doing it right, moving through the world in the right way, we will experience these synchronous moments in which things appear serendipitous and fall into place like tumblers aligning to open a lock, revealing a clearer picture. Call it flow, luck, or the perfect day, it occasionally happens to all of us—but what if it could happen much more than occasionally? As Dyer suggested, do we intentionally create this doorway and walk into synchronous flow, or do we discover it and walk through? Either way, he seems to suggest the best way to meet change starts with you, from within. What is this right way to move through our personal and professional world, and how can we organize the dual aspect of our mind to do so with efficiency, productivity, and contentment?

Structures in the Mind

When I was a kid, my neighborhood park had a geodesic dome made of steel triangles. Like a giant skeletal igloo, it was the perfect structure for climbing, walking on, weaving in and out of, and hanging from. Its frame bounded me within a defined space and at the same time gave me the freedom to experience, explore, and express myself. I spent many afternoons playing on it until it was time to come in for dinner. By contrast, mental and conceptual structures can be funny things. We rebel against them, yet we need them—sometimes wanting them desperately in our lives. With too much structure, we fall into a pit of helplessness, hopelessness, and paralysis; with too little, our feedback loops become akin to stepping off the curb into city traffic.

Why do we live in a world which either seems completely chaotic and out of control or increasingly imposes more structure and tighter constraint? And why do we routinely take steps to constrain achievement in ourselves and others, pulling others toward tightly structured means? The answer in part is because these are unconscious activities of the rational and intuitive mind.

Our realities are driven by these activities, and they're hopelessly (and wonderfully) knotted together. The good news is we needn't concern ourselves with trying to untie these knots or control them. Instead, we need to know more about the various on-ramps, off-ramps, and cloverleafs of thought they create, which direction they would take us, who we want in the driver's seat of our mind at any given moment, and what corresponding behavior is warranted. Once these considerations have been assessed, we simply need to choose our next highway and take the exit.

Up to now you may have considered things like synchronous events as random chance or simple tricks of the mind, pure subjectivity with no link to the real, and completely out of our control. But it would be more accurate to think of them as indicators of the rational and intuitive (exploitative and explorative) sides of the mind working in sync, and this reality is created by you.

We could look at constructs like rational-exploitative and intuitive-explorative thought, human reality, and synchronous moments in terms of quantum mechanics or some yet defined science. We could think of them as a simple function of hyper-awareness or acute noticing, and if so, reference back to the argument that it's a simple trick. But my advice would be to think of them both ways. The point is there is something significant going on here and it does involve awareness, noticing, balance, and a kind of "physics of the mind"—and it is significant enough to warrant reflection, as it is a part of our constructed reality, socially, professionally, and personally. The next chapter dives deeper down the rabbit hole and delves into the rational and intuitive exploitative and explorative parts of the mind and how they create and inform the world we ultimately create.

Crossroads of Cognition: Managing Paradigms and Ways of Knowing Using Ambidexterity

Do you actively *think* or merely rearrange your prejudices, biases, and judgments? Most of us do the latter. Ambidextrous organizations don't needlessly cling to old paradigms simply because someone says, "that's the way we do things around here." They continually search for new ones to adopt, they create them, and they continually challenge the ones they have. Being ambidextrous requires attention to detail, awareness, strength, focus, and an ability to change paradigms. It sounds tough but it's not difficult.

An organization has to be a "learning organization," which as we have discussed is not to be confused with organizational learning. It must have a special kind of culture, a special kind of structure, and a special kind of leadership—all built on a flexible foundation—and requires courage and emotionally intelligent left- and right-brained thinkers.

Paradigms

When a paradigm shifts, everyone and everything in the old paradigm go back to zero; this happens to people as well as organizations. Actually, it must happen to the people in the organization before the organization can make a shift, and in both cases it can have a profound effect. In the case of companies like Kodak, Xerox, and Blockbuster, the effect was profoundly bad. Kodak engineers were the first to invent the digital camera but were dismissed by management and leadership, and eventually other companies developed the same technology, getting to the market quicker. Xerox had all but created the infrastructure for an early home computer with a mouse and common computer features we are familiar with today but was so preoccupied with its copiers that it subsequently allowed its engineers, inventions, and knowledge capital to be purchased and spirited away by Steve Jobs. Most of us know what happened to Blockbuster Video and VHS tapes at the hands of companies like Netflix with DVDs, mail order, and then internet video distribution when they failed to pay attention and adapt to a changing market.

But this is not to say that everyone is affected badly when a paradigm changes. Those people and organizations who have learned to keep an open mind, those who have the foresight and courage to walk out to the edge of an existing paradigm and peer over get a glimpse of what is coming next (emerging) and are able to prepare themselves for the changes of the next big thing, and sometimes create the next big thing.

What are paradigms? Think of them as roadmaps or navigational compass headings. Akin to schema, they are familiar and vetted patterns, mental models, frameworks, and shortcuts we create to save time, work more efficiently, and exploit what we already know—and, yes, paradigms contain prejudices, biases, and judgments. As Steven Covey said in *The 7 Habits of Highly Effective People,* paradigms are subjective, as each of us perceives and understands the world in our own way. No one is really an objective observer, and paradigms can be positive or negative. With that said, as long as we are walking within the realm of the familiar and using our paradigms with thoughtful intent, they're benevolent, helpful, and work great. But venture beyond them into new territory or use them carelessly, and we find ourselves lost and without a useable strategy.

Schema

When I started my research, my expectation was that finding ambidexterity in a company would be like finding a unicorn, but I was wrong. I found to my surprise that all companies start out ambidextrous but then quickly change. What I discovered was that *few* organizations were able to sustain *ambidextrous* behavior; this was the real unicorn. The results of 40 years of research on the subject of organizational ambidexterity were right: *Exploitation drives out exploration.* As organizations learn to do something well, they repeat those processes and subsequently stop learning new things, at least not in *revolutionary* ways. Slow, incremental *evolutionary* learning might happen but not the big jumps, pivots, and paradigm shifts that represent rapid growth and learning. Organizations become one-trick ponies and effectively stamp an expiration date upon their foreheads and begin winding down or lagging behind.

What is the catalyzing link between ambidexterity and paradigms? For one thing, ambidexterity challenges paradigms and evokes *schema*. It causes organizations and people to exercise their traditional routines, test out their long-held assumptions and mental checklists, and actively consider whether those are still serving them in optimal ways for a given moment. When we discover a roadblock in the execution of an old paradigm, we are momentarily confronted with new learning and must consider new pathways and processes if we're going to continue. When considering completely new frameworks, learning becomes more permanent when tethered to the familiar, if only loosely. This provides us with the confidence, courage, and sensemaking to step off the ledge of the familiar and into the completely unfamiliar by providing an overlay template we create which says "this is sort of like 'X,' and I know how to do that"; this is schema. A short YouTube video titled *Schema*[34] by brainrulesbook illustrates this phenomenon very nicely.

Sensemaking

Often we are so wedded to our paradigms as adults because they help us make sense of an uncertain world. They are like flashlights in the dark, navigational maps of cognition that get us from one place to another and from one thought to another. Without them, we would be paralyzed, afraid, or both. In a recent conversation, a friend commented that an ambidextrous organization reminded him of childhood in that we begin navigating through life by building and piggybacking on the paradigms of family and friends and walk through new experiences for the first time to make our own. When new learning occurs, we learn, or relearn, lessons through skinned knees or stories from others, through failure, success, embarrassment, or triumph. It's all potential grist for the mill, and through crying, laughing, observing, and reflecting, we build our own paradigms to assist us in our execution of life. Some of them we use like bicycles, employing them daily; we lock some of them down and don't deviate from their original checklist steps—going to church or doing daily chores, for example.

---

[34] https://www.youtube.com/watch?v=mzbRpMlEHzM

Others we avoid after experiencing them once, hoping to never revisit them, perhaps for the rest of our lives. We develop an appetite for favorite paradigms and a distaste for others and can assign negative and positive feelings to them.

Someone once said that life is not what happens to you but instead how you react to what happens. If you get lost in a strange city, you could see it as a frustrating, unproductive failure or an adventurous opportunity to discover a new city. The difference will be in the paradigms you have created and use for such a circumstance. The point is this: How we create and utilize paradigms is a choice, and this in turn depends on how we order, make sense of, and view the world. While the proper utilization of created paradigms is critical, it's important to understand what they're made of in order to use them to their full potential.

What is sensemaking? Researcher Karl Weick in *Sensemaking in Organizations* (1995) called sensemaking quite simply the making of sense. It involves such things as comprehension, making meaning, placing items into frameworks, redressing surprise, patterning, and interaction in pursuit of mutual understanding. So, while a paradigm is your executed direction and destination on a map, sensemaking is what you pick up along the route; it's what happens to you along the way, how you use what you collect and even what meaning you get from it. This in turn informs and feeds your paradigms.

It's important to clarify that paradigms, schema, and sensemaking are important tools in a toolbox, but not oracles reporting some absolute truth. First, they're very personal, and second, they're designed to get us down the road and around the bend to a vantage point where we can see a clearer picture and inform the next step. They're not explicit instructions. In one of several powerful stories about sensemaking, Weick discussed an army regiment on maneuvers in the Swiss Alps in winter that was feared lost during a snowstorm. Not familiar with the mountain range, the soldiers had lost hope of return and become disheartened until one of them produced a map from his coat pocket. Encouraged by the map, they set up camp and waited out the storm. During that time they mainly discussed their orientation, reflected on their steps, shared cues, and felt confident they knew the way out. The next day, they marched out of the mountains. When they returned to the base, they told their story to their commandant and produced the saving map. Upon study of it, the commandant discovered it was not a map of the Alps; it was in fact a map of the Pyrenees. They had used a map of the Pyrenees mountains to find their way out of the Alps. The map, albeit wrong, had provided the cues and sensemaking needed for them to find the right answer, proving that when you're lost any old map will do. What this illustrates is that data and answers don't always have to be absolute or perfect; arguably, in some instances they may never be. They just have to generate better questions, which lead to better actions.

In this way, ambidextrous organizations behave differently. Organizations like Google, Toyota, Zappos, 3M, and others are great examples. They have adopted a different model, one built on asking better and better questions that move them in a synergistic upward spiral. They follow biology and principles like *negative entropy* (the breathing in and out of living organisms) and consider the principles and language of quantum physics instead of only Newtonian physics and industrialism from the turn of the last century. Their model leverages the best of what the world and humanity currently offer—diversity in all areas; abundance of available disparate, common, and overlooked knowledge which litters the hallways of most organizations; increased consciousness; and new advances in technology and science—instead of simply relying on what's been successful in the past.

Stories and Perspective

Stories inform and teach us lessons in ways data alone cannot. One of the most powerful stories I have told over the years teaches the lesson of not "zooming in" the aperture of perception concerning reality, particularly if you're in a leadership position, and the power of words. Though it may feel sensible and even comforting to do so, it may create an inertia in your organization's culture that would be hard to pull away from or change and keep you from seeing incredible new opportunities right in front of you.

In the 1880s there was an American company that made wooden buckets. The artisans and craftsmen in this company were so proud of the quality buckets they made for various uses that they wanted their company to be called a wooden bucket company to highlight their craftsmanship. The owner, however, had another idea: he chose instead to characterize the company as a "container" company. This proved to be a wise move. Eventually, through advances in technology, the landscape began to change and wood became obsolete. The new medium was now glass. Because the company was a "container" company, it easily made the technological jump from wood to glass and was able to compete in the market. Years later, technology changed again to plastic, and the company began making plastic containers. The company later made metal containers and branched out into aerospace. This company is the Ball company, a billion-dollar organization originally famous for its mason jars used for canning. Because the original founders refused to characterize themselves and what they did in the narrow margins of the day, they have been able to make sense of new technology, innovation, and opportunities for over 130 years.

10

Stress and Control, Consciousness and Reality

"Between fight and flight is the blind man's sight and the choice that's right." –Jewel

I don't know the origin of the expression "blind man's sight," but I think pop and country singer Jewel Kilcher captures its meaning beautifully in the lyrics from her 2001 song "Standing Still." The visible world can be a shockingly pervasive, in-your-face experience. Consequently, it distracts, confuses, challenges, sometimes terrifies, and occupies virtually every moment of our waking lives. With one of our senses removed, you might think our mind would have a better chance at thinking clearly and processing reality more accurately, helping us make "the choice that's right," but you'd be wrong. As Jewel hints, there is another layer of noise to contend with if we remove sight: the noise within our heads. Even when we can filter out the external world, we are left with an often stressful internal world within our mind. In order to get the best picture of life, it's imperative to know who's giving you advice, learn self-control, and understand a few things about consciousness before you can think about picking best choices.

In the ambidextrous world of organizations (the world of *exploitative* and *explorative* practices), it's imperative to find balance.

If you don't, you'll stamp an expiration date upon your head and eventually go extinct. Forty years of research on the subject backs this up, saying that exploitation drives out exploration. What this means is most organizations converge on one or two things they've learned to do well, stop growing, learning, and changing, and eventually go extinct when the environment changes. Just as organizations get out of balance, so do people. So, unless you want to squander your best years like a sad character in a Leo Tolstoy novel or find, as Thomas Merton said, "your ladder leaning against the wrong wall," you'll want to consider this section carefully and adjust your balance, and reality, accordingly.

The last chapter started a conversation around understanding exploitative and explorative balance in the mind and the linkages to the outside world. This chapter continues the conversation and introduces fundamental reasons why hurdles to achieving optimal states of consciousness (reality) exist, where they come from, and ways to get over them in our lives. The thing about hurdles is this: Though they may at first look like permanent obstructions, they're actually moveable structures. Once mastered, they can be easily kicked down and reduced to mere pebbles in the road.

Know What Part of Your Brain Is Giving You Advice

The oldest part of our brain, the amygdala, is 300 million years old and handles basic functioning. The amygdala knows four things—I call them the four "F's"—*fight, flight, food,* and, for the sake of being civil, *fornicate.* This primordial brain is all early humans needed to keep themselves out of trouble, keep them fed, and continue the bloodline. Then 100 million years ago came the *limbic* brain, which brought with it emotion and short-term memory, and 3 million years ago came the *prefrontal cortex,* giving us consciousness and higher-order thinking.

In our 21st century world, when you go about your daily activities, the different parts of the brain check in with help and advice. Just because you left a meeting in a glass and chrome office building or flew in an airplane across the country, you may think you're getting information drawn exclusively from the higher-functioning part of the brain (the prefrontal cortex), but this would not be the case. You're actually taking counsel from all parts of the brain, old and new, and one of the loudest advocates is the ever-vigilant amygdala.

Do you ever feel as if there's a war going on inside your head? Well, there is: That's the amygdala and the prefrontal cortex fighting. While this part of our brain works 24/7 to keep us out of trouble, it's also at a disadvantage today. The amygdala was created to cope with a different environment millions of years ago, what psychologists call the "immediate return environment." In the amygdala's world, spears are flung from rival tribes and sabre-toothed cats leap from rock faces above, regardless of what the current 21st century situation might be. It's a world of startle and response; everything is going to kill you, and everything requires immediate action. And then just as quickly as it started, to the amygdala it's over. By contrast, the environment of today is known as a "delayed return environment." We now live in a world where cause and effect, and action and response, can take longer and are usually non–life-threatening, though we still feel as though losing our job or blowing an important presentation may result in certain death, and the farther out the potential threat, the harder it is for the amygdala to see it.

And it gets even better. As if to add insult to injury, our primordial brain is completely blind to the 21st century emergencies it should be alerting us about. We all know people who have no problem using tobacco and other carcinogenic substances or participating in repetitively detrimental habits like overeating, worrying, and dubious lifestyle activities. Where is the cautious amygdala in these instances? It's silent and oblivious, yet these are the sabre-toothed cats of our day. So Jewel is right: We are often pinned between feelings of wanting to attack or run away. Combine this with a world that feels ominously dangerous, which we don't know how to instinctively respond to in helpful ways, and you've got stress. What can we do about it? One answer is "biohacking."

In the book *Game Changers*,[35] Dave Asprey explained how to overcome unhelpful patterns of behavior that hold us back and get the body and mind working together by updating our personal operating system's default settings that control the nervous system. Techniques like avoiding decision fatigue, taking control of our diet, adjusting sleep schedules, and quelling undefined fear are a few examples of how to edit long-established default settings using biohacking. Fear and worry have many negative effects. While some stress is good for the body, sustained fear triggers stress, which releases chemicals like cortisol. Long-term release of cortisol corrodes the nervous system, effectively oxidizing the body. Fear also consumes large amounts of energy, a finite resource. Additionally, fear discourages us from taking risks that could otherwise lead to our success. To the primordial mind, a risk is a gamble that if gone wrong could lead to failure, and failure in prehistoric times often meant death. As a result, we are hard wired (defaulted) to be ill disposed to failure. We can overcome fear with courage, but courage, again, requires energy (effort), a finite resource. Adding up the problems that come along with a fearful amygdala can leave us with an exhausted, unfocused, and risk-averse mind. Furthermore, Asprey said the subconscious mind doesn't just want us to find an absence of threats to feel safe; it also wants to find confirmation of safety.

You Are Not Your Brain; You Are the User of Your Brain

This advice comes from one of my heroes, Rudy Tanzi.[36] A small group of neuroscientists has moved beyond the reductionist view that our brains are nothing more than synapses firing and electrochemical processes, and leading Alzheimer's researcher Rudy is one of them. He's courageously exploring the nature of human consciousness and reality in his neuroscience research.

The newest part of our brain, the prefrontal cortex, gives us consciousness and higher-order thinking. It also gives us the ability

---

[35] https://www.aspreygamechangers.com/
[36] https://en.wikipedia.org/wiki/Rudolph_E._Tanzi

to stand outside of ourselves and witness what's going on without instinctively getting caught up in it and immediately reacting. This part of our brain gives us empathy and the advantage of standing back and assessing situations, provided the amygdala doesn't attempt to intervene. As Rudy explained, "You *have* a brain, but you are *not* your brain." You are the owner of your brain; it doesn't own you. That's an important point to remember. Similar to Rudy's explanation, I like to think of the brain as a faithful dog. As such, it should be nurtured and loved, walked, fed, trained, let out to run at times and kept on a leash at others—oh, and keep it out of your neighbors' trash and from getting in fights with skunks and other dogs.

Perhaps most compelling of all, Rudy said the only job of our brain is to create. We create thoughts, deeds, words, facial expressions, artwork, etc., and that which we create ultimately comes back to govern, regulate, and monitor us. Consciousness, Rudy said, is simply awareness. More specifically, it's "awareness of our own awareness" in an amazing amount of feedback loops.[37] Pull something into your noticing awareness—a tree, a coffee mug, a blue sky, whatever—and now you're creating reality!

---

[37] Tanzi, R. (2014). Evolution of the brain, consciousness and lucid dreaming. https://www.youtube.com/watch?v=5LKFOiC8wag

11

Achieving Balance in the Workplace

The last chapter addressed the human mind with the introduction of hurdles—hurdles that keep us from achieving control and balance and create negative stressors on our work and personal lives. This chapter continues the discussion with more hurdles to ambidextrous balance, productivity, and happiness. Why is it important to address organizational ambidexterity and balancing of exploitation and exploration at the individual level? Think of scaling and neuroscience. When we think of scaling a business, we think of growth. Scaling ambidexterity is not much different, only it's tied to a company's culture, performance, and strategic health.

In the introduction to this book I introduced the three types of organizational ambidexterity: *temporal*, *structural*, and *contextual*. Scaling up ambidexterity from individuals to an organization brings the highest form of ambidexterity into the organization, *contextual*, because it starts with the well-balanced individual. On a neuroscience level, we are all watchers, observing, picking up on, and mimicking the behavior of those around us. Mirror neurons in the brain take care of this and naturally cause us to imitate the behavior of others. The more balanced high-performing individuals you have, the more likely it is you will also have these characteristics at the organizational level, creating a healthier culture.

A Word About Balance, Happiness, and Mindfulness

Before we go further, I feel it's important for me to say a few words about *balance, happiness*, and *mindfulness*. I do this particularly to quell any potential uprisings from my left-brained exploitatively disposed readership who might think I've abandoned them or that I'm getting soft. I am firmly in the middle and moderate in my beliefs for a "middle road," balanced, even stoic path of practicing both *exploitative* and *explorative* behavior, which would not consider one thing without also looking closely at its opposite. I also believe *movement* is good; an organization that is static is also stagnant, dead, or dying. Companies must breathe in and out like living organisms (with negative entropy) in order to continuously renew and refresh themselves. So, any talk of balance in these conversations is not a talk of stillness. It has more to do with surfing an optimal edge between chaos and calm, and between exploitation and exploration, than it does with operating in a static state; it's a model in perpetual motion.

Next, stress, challenge, chaos, and even moments of discomfort (unhappiness) are good things for people and companies to experience with the right mindset. These experiences stretch, challenge, and show us alternative realities. Even failure helps us learn and grow. In fact, studies have proven people are happier when they experience occasional periods of unhappiness. Numerous books like *A Guide to the Good Life, The Upside of Stress, The Happiness Advantage, Rewire,* and *Loving What Is* suggest practicing things like "voluntary discomfort" and attest that stress, which occurs when something we care about is at stake, is bad only if we think it is. Stress doesn't come from an event but from our interpretation of that event. What this means is if we change our interpretation of an event to a more positive one, the accompanying stress can be beneficial; our positivity affects our health, and happy lives contain stress. Conversely, negative emotions constrict our ability to think and act and release all sorts of chemicals into the body and mind which, with frequency and negative perspective, can damage us.

Mindfulness, and even *mindlessness,* also deserve respect and consideration as they help us order and optimize our conscious experiences and promote creative breakthroughs. Mindless (subconscious) processing has more computing power available than the conscious mind, as the unconscious mind accounts for as much as 90% of our mental processing. This is why good ideas and solutions to problems often come after a night's rest. So, to put my conscious, exploitative, left-brained, frontal cortex, objectively thinking advocates at ease, I'm not abandoning you. No one could be more passionate about the rational side of human thought than I am, especially in this age. I am simply trying to give the silent, intuitive, explorative right-brained side equal voice. As quoted earlier, Albert Einstein said, "The intuitive mind is a sacred gift and the rational mind is a faithful servant. We have created a society that has honored the servant but forgotten the gift." We have also created organizations that have forgotten. Ambidexterity is about restoring this balance and tapping into this powerful resource. Let's look at how to continue creating the best balanced you!

Embrace New Physics

None of us would dream of trying to defy the laws of classical physics by jumping off a building without some type of deceleration device like a parachute, right? So why do we keep ignoring and attempting to circumvent our newest form of physics, quantum physics? The most logical answer is because we don't know any better and we are habitually social creatures. We currently live in a world that reveres classical physics as gospel yet treats quantum physics with ignorant aloofness; however, this picture is beginning to change.

As I was writing this book, a longtime engineer friend from San Diego mentioned a book written in the 1970s called the *Tao of Physics.*[38] After reading it, I realized he had given me a gift, an

---

[38] Capra, F. (2010). *Tao of physics: An exploration of the parallels between modern physics and Eastern mysticism.* https://www.amazon.com/Tao-Physics-Exploration-Parallels-Mysticism/p/1590308352

important piece of the jigsaw puzzle the universe seemed to be nudging me to construct. Classical physics, a science expressed through the precise and rational language of mathematics, strives to *measure, quantify, classify*, and *analyze* material reality in the pursuit of objective knowledge (truth). This is to say, the classical physics formulated by Newton is based on ideas like *absolute space and time*, the *existence of elementary solid particles*, the notion *you can determine the behavior of physical objects*, and the view that nature can be described objectively regardless of an observer's perspective. Modern physics, largely conceived by Einstein, contradicts these concepts by putting forth the notion that the movements of sub-atomic particles can't be determined with certainty but rather show *tendencies* to occur. Furthermore, objective descriptions of nature are impossible since atomic particles are affected by the very act of their observation. This is a game-changing revelation.

As discussed earlier in this book, when these quantum rules are introduced in the organizational world, they are consistently ignored with a kind of arrogance. This is to say, leaders, managers, and employees won't consider *tendencies* in favor of making what they think are accurate objective determinations in a *non-deterministic* world. This contradiction makes perfect sense, as we all would like to snap a chalk line on things and be done with them, but people, processes, and nature cannot be handled in such a way. How do we get over this hurdle? First, we must stop going against these laws by trying to create deterministic outcomes and then attempting to control them. Instead, we must summon the courage and patience to be comfortable in a world where we don't always have the full picture when we want it, as that's not how the quantum universe works. It's more apt to show us the (current) correct answer in its own time after we have filtered distractions, calmed our fears and anxiety, and asked the right questions of ourselves and others. Once the answer comes, it should be understood that the only control we will have is in the way in which we interpret and react to it. Neuroscientist Rudy Tanzi said the job of the human mind is to create; we are creation machines, but we can't control.[39] Control, he said, comes from self-organization and is the job of the universe; try to do that job and you may go extinct. Henry Mintzberg once told me that middle managers were destroying organizations with their meddling, and Karl Weick said they often cause problems by interfering with "self-correcting" processes. That's quantum physics being ignored! If the only job of the mind is to create, be thoughtfully deliberate in your creations, then sit back and see how the universe organizes it for you.

Find Your Flow

Find your flow, and find it quickly! I don't say this to alarm you, and I'm certainly not implying you are late to the race and should have known what you've wanted to be and do from day one. What I am saying is you should actively be searching for it now. The sooner you find out what puts you into a "flow state" and start incorporating those activities into your daily routine, the happier and more successful you'll be. What is flow? The concept originated with psychologist Mihaly Csikszentmihalyi (pronounced "Me-Hi Cheek-Sent-Me-Hi"), and while it may seem unfamiliar, we've all experienced it. There's another term for flow associated with sports which will help you recognize it: *in the zone.*

The concept goes like this. There's a channel of productive activity between the feeling of being challenged and being skilled at something. In this channel, we experience a blissful state in which we lose track of time. No doubt we all remember playing as children and having to be called in to the house multiple times because we were so engrossed in activities that we forgot everything else. That's flow. With too much challenge, we become anxious, even panicked, but with too little we become bored or disinterested. To be in the flow channel is to be in the "sweet spot," the optimal place of activity in which we are focused and engulfed in what we're doing. How do you find flow? If you can identify

---

[39] Tanzi, R. (2014). Evolution of the brain, consciousness and lucid dreaming. https://www.youtube.com/watch?v=5LKFOiC8wag

your passions in life, what it is you would you do if you had all the money in the world, there's where you'll find flow. Author Sally Hogshead said it another way: Find your "fascination advantage" and you will find flow.[40] Hogshead says there are seven fascination advantages people possess related to personality traits. Find yours and there you will find flow.

Muster Courage

In the recently released movie *The Green Book*, the main character was asked why a gifted genius would take so many risks with his otherwise comfortable and accomplished life. His reply? "Possessing genius is nothing without also having courage." That's our next barrier. Many brilliant people walking among us could make game-changing contributions to their organizations, their lives, and humanity if they could muster courage. There are different reasons why they don't do this—societal influence, lack of stamina or energy, and of course the primal brain warning us against risk taking. An old Chinese proverb says, "The nail that sticks up gets hammered down." However, if these people wouldn't give in to the warnings from their brain, they might find themselves living their very best lives. Here's the rub: Without first questioning and reflecting on advice given, even and especially our own, we'll be led around by the nose by well-meaning yet ignorant, fearful advisers. What's the solution? Have the courage to ask questions like you did when you were a child. Buckminster Fuller once said, "Everyone is born a genius but the act of living *de-geniuses* us." Muster your courage and you will reconnect with your genius, and maybe even your inner child!

Living the Dream

At the beginning of this discussion, I said it's difficult to filter the outside world and experience a reality void of distraction.

---

[40] Hogshead, S. (2016). *Fascinate, revised and updated: How to make your brand impossible to resist.* https://www.amazon.com/gp/product/B011IT59WU/ref=dbs_a_def_rwt_hsch_vapi_tkin_p1_i0

However, when we sleep at night, it's perhaps the one time we have a chance to slip the bonds of Earth and experience an alternative reality without external distraction. I ran into my local drugstore yesterday to pick up a few things and passed by a clerk sitting cross-legged on the floor stocking a shelf. As he looked up acknowledging me, I offered a greeting and a "how's it going?" His reply was brilliant: "Just living the dream!" This immediately took me back, giving me pause. The first time I heard that expression made popular by the film *Top Gun*, I was a sergeant flying as a crewmember aboard Air Force 2. Our missions on Air Force 2 and in support of Air Force 1 were at times exciting and at others either extremely stressful or dull. For us, repeating the mantra "living the dream" to one another became a sort of comforting affirmation and meditation, designed to psych ourselves up from the anxiety or boredom we were about to experience and change our mental attitude in a positive way—and it always worked. My clerk friend was undoubtedly practicing the same technique to get through his current situation.

But what if there's more to this saying than we realize? Are we really experiencing a form of reality (life) when we dream? And more importantly, what if we can "live out" our dreams while awake? When we sleep, we mute the external world and experience a world inside our mind. If we consider the definition of human consciousness (reality), we *do* experience another form of conscious reality at night, and this world is also a real one. Human consciousness as defined is *awareness* and proven out (verified and validated) by the accounting of a reportable experience. Remembered dreams are reportable experiences and as such meet the criterion for consciousness (reality). While sometimes amazing, impossible, fantastic, shocking, and drastically different from the reality you're experiencing as you read this, the unencumbered dream world is every bit as real as our waking reality.

My point is this: Perhaps Tom Cruise, my Air Force crewmates, and most recently my store clerk friend are right—we do have the ability to "live" our dreams, whatever we might dream, and dare them to be. What can we do with these two worlds—the inside world of our mind and the outside external world—that together make up life? Simple, overlay the maps, integrate and stitch the two worlds together. Coalesce the outside world with the inside and then surf the edge of that wave for your best reality!

12

Authenticity

"So I'm a little left of center, I'm a little out of tune. Some say I'm paranormal, so I just bend their spoon. Who wants to be ordinary, in a crazy mixed up world." —Michelle Branch

Michelle Branch's catchy 2001 song "You Get Me" has it right: Nobody wants to be ordinary. Yet society, our employers, peers, and even our loved ones seem to beckon us toward average. Eventually, most of us conceal or lose track of our authentic selves behind a cloak of ordinary and conform to what we think others want from us. However, the actual truth is we are certainly *not* ordinary, not in any way and not any one of us. Instead of squelching our uniqueness and authentic selves, individuals, organizations, and society should be celebrating and encouraging it. We should be actively searching for the ways in which we are different; the world needs our uniqueness.

Earlier in the book, we talked about creating a more balanced you, and the last part of that equation is being your authentic self, providing the best you can muster for your organizations, yourself, your family, and humanity. Why? Because ambidextrous organizations (AOs), those that can both *exploit* and *explore* with equal success, are at their core (their culture) authentic, and at the core of your company's culture is you. Most importantly, a genuine *you* gives an entire organization permission to also be authentic.

I saw a movie that had a powerful message—*Glass* by M. Night Shyamalan. In it, a secret society monitored and controlled people who believed they had "super powers," a superhero or supervillain delusion. This delusional grandeur, however, was not delusional. In the movie, for the good of humanity, the secret society worked to suppress individuals who possessed superhuman abilities. In chapter 8, I told the story of Icarus and discussed governors we put on ourselves and that others impose upon us. In other chapters, I discussed the nature of reality and redefined consciousness. As Buckminster Fuller said, we're all born geniuses but the act of living "de-geniuses'" us. Being your authentic self means finding and reconnecting with your genius, your superpowers, and the unique qualities and abilities you possess and sharing them with the world. Though there may not be true superheroes among us like in the movie, the world has and continues to see remarkable individuals who achieve remarkable feats. Think of athletes like Jim Thorpe, recent Olympic medal winner Michael Phelps, Daniel Tammet who recited pi from memory to 22,514 digits, and Buddhist monks who alter their body temperature with their minds. People with unique abilities are all around us, and one of them is you.

The Authentic Self

Whenever I'm in the city, I love to run. It's always an energizing, visceral, and rewarding experience. One morning not long ago, I was fortunate enough to go on a run through the city with my cousin, son, and brother-in-law. I was in my element and able to be my authentic self. It was a real experience with people I care about who also care about me. I'll never forget it! What is authenticity like in the workplace? It's a little like my run on that spring day.

Author Mike Robbins says authenticity is not about honesty but about realness; it's an "in the moment" phenomenon and includes things like vulnerability, humility, courage, individuality, knowing yourself and your personality.[41] Authenticity is also contagious; practicing it gives others permission to be real. Robbins

---

[41] Robbins, M. (2013). The power of authenticity. https://www.youtube.com/watch?v=d4iFAAUscVA

Running with my cousin, son, and brother-in-law in Washington, DC.

warned, however, that authenticity is not an excuse to be rude, outrageous, or detrimental; far from getting you praised, such behavior might damage your career.

In discussing authenticity, researcher Caroline McHugh said that "individuality *is* everything it's cracked up to be."[42] She said authentic people are larger than life and shine as if they swallowed the moon. We all know people like this, and their personalities draw us in like a moth to a flame. McHugh said society "archetypes" us around the age of 6 or 7, and this reinforces our developing consciousness; it also introduces self-consciousness. As a result, we become less good at being ourselves. Authentic people, however, have figured out their one true gift. She said your job is to be good at being you; you can't be anyone else. Interestingly, McHugh discussed two classic complexes that are signs of a fragile ego and offered a third of her own design as a healthier alternative.

Interiority. McHugh said an *inferiority* complex comes when you suffer from an over-modest self-regard, while *superiority* is

---

[42] McHugh, C. (2013). The art of being yourself. https://www.youtube.com/watch?v=veEQQ-N9xWU

when you think you're the most important person in the room. One complex is about delusions of insignificance, while the other is about delusions of grandeur; both require the cooperative participation of others. In one, you need people to find you out (for the imposter you really are), while in the other, people around you need to be smaller so that you can feel superior. An *interiority complex*, by comparison, is a third way of being in the world and offers a perceptual vantage point and a sensibility. It's an orientation that is not related to others and the only place in your life McHugh said you have no competition, as it's not possible to find an exact comparison to yourself. While it's impossible to be perception-less, such an orientation allows you to be perception-free. Without it, there are as many opinions of you as there are people, and you could spend a lifetime searching for yourself in the conjecture of others, never finding you. Operating from interiority is a liberating way to live authentically, said McHugh.

Ego. A big part of authenticity is managing ego. We all need an ego, and McHugh said your whole life has been about building a more stable relationship with it. Superiority, inferiority—our ego takes us to extremes, disrupting our lives and endeavors by cueing us up to an outside world rather than an inside compass. Authenticity is about taking your ego from its dominant position and putting it in the service of you. Develop a position that's impervious to both good and bad, to anything!

What if organizations could have the same effect authentic people do? If they could draw us in with their magnetic allure, would we run to work there? Would it profoundly change us?

The Authentic Organization

Is authenticity important for organizations to have? Rohit Bhargavam said yes, companies need personality,[43] yet many organizations—including most of them in the field I'm in—still

---

[43] Bhargave, R. (2008). *Personality not included: Why companies lose their authenticity and how great brands get it back.* https://www.amazon.com/Personality-Not-Included-Companies-Authenticity/dp/0071545212

think companies should be faceless, or at the very least "personality-less." This kind of thinking is outdated, however, and the picture is changing even more against this mindset as we move further into the digital and artificial intelligence economies. Customers no longer want to interface with companies and people pretending to be automatons, especially since they're interfacing with real automatons with increasing frequency. Additionally, employees no longer want to feel like they're a voiceless part of a machine as they realize working without authenticity is, well, inauthentic and reduces them to the status of a commodity.

Spokespeople. Organizations have traditionally feared personality and authenticity because they believe it will destroy any air of success or trustworthiness they have, said Bhargava. However, to create a true bond with customers, you must give your company a voice, and employees should be empowered to be spokespeople, feeling confident in expressing their company's vision. When openly able to talk about their passion, individuals energize themselves, inspire others (mirror neutrons), and build on the credibility of the company. The accidental spokesperson, who catches the "authenticity bug," will enthusiastically herald the organization's message—for free! This is probably the most vivid and real voice a brand could hope for. An organization will never have this opportunity without first allowing authenticity.

Lateral thinkers. Bhargava said most companies are also afraid of lateral thinkers who come up with ideas that challenge or change current practices. So, instead of encouraging their employees to think outside the box, they urge them to follow instructions and fall in line. It's essential to avoid this kind of thinking because the image of the company relies not just on how employees do their jobs but also about how they feel about their jobs. If a company discourages authenticity and employees become automatons, it will be reflected in the company's image, culture, and identity. Rather than having believable spokespeople, there will be only a few carefully vetted appointees with a high-gloss, watered down, or disingenuous message.

Engagement. Here's the bottom line: An organization can't have it both ways. It can't have engaged, authentic people and then dictate the terms of their engagement and authenticity. Author Price Pritchett cited a Gallup poll which said that only 15% of employees worldwide are engaged in their jobs.[44] Pritchett said the best employee engagement program is one driven by employees' own self-interest. What does this mean? It means employees may have signed on with the organization to do a specific job, but they want to do it their way provided they give the organization desired results. And they want to develop their careers in their own way too, developing their authentic selves. What can support like this do for an organization? For one thing, it represents future investment; an organization is likely to have engaged and happy employees.

Commodities. Once you learn who you are and get comfortable with your authentic self, the first thing you will notice is relief because you will realize you are no longer replaceable. Sure, you could be physically replaced, but they won't get another you and your coworkers and employer will know this. What's a commodity? It's an article of trade or commerce, a product. Commodities are valuable things we need and depend on, but they should never be people. Commodities are replaceable, consumable, unremarkable from one another, and plentiful. Think about McDonald's restaurants and their products; they're the same the world over and you don't have any preference as to which one you might visit for a cheeseburger. When people allow themselves to become cheeseburgers, either by volition or because their organization treats them like commodities, just like the paper cups at McDonalds, they become replaceable. Don't be a cheeseburger.

The why and how. Why do organizations do this? They most likely fear losing something (market share, control, customer trust), or perhaps they think if they standardize their workforce the way they have their products, they will have a more efficient business.

---

[44] Pritchett, P. (2012). *The employee handbook of new work habits for a radically changing world.* https://www.amazon.com/Employee-Handbook-Habits-Radically-Changing/dp/0944002153

How do they do it? By choking individual personality and authenticity and promoting arbitrary one-size-fits-all policies. When you take humanity out of business, what kind of business are you left with? Zappos, the online shoe and clothing retailer, promotes what it calls "work/ life integration" in an effort to integrate their employees' professional and personal lives. Additionally, the company encourages individuality, the pursuit of pleasure at work, and even "weirdness" in their workforce, i.e., authenticity.

The reunion of humanity and business. When organizations inadvertently or intentionally turn people away from authenticity, they begin down a slippery slope and find themselves with all manner of undiagnosed maladies that erode organizational culture, identity, and performance. Friend and researcher Rob Bogosian knows these ills all too well. An expert on cultures of voice and cultures of silence, Rob said that when organizations go silent, it's a bad sign and can indicate problems ranging from issues of psychological safety to apathy.[45] I haven't discussed a correlation between authenticity and organizational voice with Rob, but I am willing to bet there's a connection. So, make yourself useful, dependable, and valuable like a commodity, but also bring your authentic self—and if you feel you can't, it might be a sign your company is not an ambidextrous organization or even capable of becoming one. It might be a sign to move on to a more courageous, productive, and authentic place. Remember this advice: Your biggest responsibility in life is to bring your authentic self to all you do; make sure it's happy and invited to the party. As the saying goes, "Go where you're celebrated, not tolerated."

---

[45] Bogosian, R., & Casper, C. M. (2014). *Breaking corporate silence: How high-influence leaders create cultures of voice.* https://rvbassociates.com/the-book/

PART IV:
CONCLUSION

13

Land Here:
Arriving at Organizational Ambidexterity

The place where the rubber meets the road is of particular interest to pilots—the reason being it is the optimal touchdown point they aim for to ensure the best chance at a safe landing. Whether the word *pilot* applies to you metaphorically or literally (I have a few pilot friends) makes little difference here; we are all pilots of our own destinies and hopefully all looking for the perfect destination and spot to land. Throughout this book, we have discussed organizational ambidexterity, the ability for companies and their people to think simultaneously in two very different ways. One way is exploitative, taking advantage of what we have already learned to do best over time, and the other way is explorative, discovering and learning new things and putting them in our toolbox as new capabilities. Together, these two ways of thinking and being represent a complete circle, a whole, meaningful, and engaged life.

We've looked at this subject from all angles, and at all levels—leadership, culture, learning, and from the individual to the group. As I close, I'll leave you with some final paradoxes, thoughts, and ideas to consider. Keep in mind, you may be the CEO of a large company or the server wiping down tables in the dining room, but either way it's the same. These ideas can benefit you and can be implemented by you. Whoever you are, you are a powerful agent for growth, innovation, fulfillment, and productivity. I suggest you consider what's here and integrate the ideas that resonate. You are the pilot of your life, and my hope is that these chapters have helped you circumnavigate dangerous storms, climb higher, find the smooth air, and land safely at your dream organization with extra fuel on board.

Here are four ideas to help you maintain the best balance of the ambidextrous organization you've built—one that equally exploits and explores, involving performing, learning, innovating, and growing, and one whose members find meaning, belonging, engagement, and purpose in the work they do and clamor with excitement to get into the building every day and work.

Recognize the Performance Paradox

We are never "doing nothing." Even when our bodies are at rest, our minds remain active, questioning, solving problems, strategizing future activities, or subconsciously crunching data and problems. Yet we are comfortable in the judgment of others and ourselves as unproductive, lazy, or inactive, particularly at work. Do we really have an appreciation for how productivity works? It's not intuitive to say one must sometimes *slow down* in order to *speed up* or that great strides can be made during periods of inactivity or diversion, but it's true regarding performance. This is the "paradox of performance." Sometimes if we want to increase performance (in the quality and sustainability of work), we need to periodically slow down, sometimes *way* down. We need to do this for different reasons: to reflect on events, allow in collaborators, and give our subconscious mind time to come up with new strategies.

I recently watched a 1950s sci-fi movie[46] that illustrated this point nicely. In the movie, a renowned entomologist (a bug guy) from the East Coast was called upon to examine the curious appearance of creatures wreaking havoc in the desert near a secret military installation. The scientist was initially given a few details as he boarded a plane for the West Coast. He had time to process and think about what he was told as he traveled. There was a written report waiting for him when he landed, and again he had

---

[46] *Them!* https://www.youtube.com/watch?v=v4URRp39XOo

additional time to reflect on the new data as he traveled to the location to get a first-hand look. The scientist eventually surmised that radiation exposure from recent nuclear testing had caused common ants to grow to the size of tour busses.

In the 24/7 culture of the 21st century, there is little allocation for "down time." Our actors built upon their knowledge gradually and had processing time between events to reflect on the last thing learned and loop that new learning into their next action. *Experience or act, reflect, repeat*—this is called "double-loop learning." If this movie were set today, the events described would transpire much differently, likely curtailing this process. This "new normal" is a serious problem, creating a frustrating *fire-ready-aim* effect, causing duplication of effort, confusion, and waste in a resource-conscious world. CEOs know organizations must perform to stay competitive, and people must work diligently and sincerely. This often means the most popular and validating assumption of the day is in the observation of continual maximum effort.

I have a very smart friend in the defense industry who commented recently, "We seem to avoid learning and thinking so we can be perceived as taking action; unfortunately, this is often meaningless and deleterious." He's right: Organizations that are more focused on being "results-oriented" perform better than those focused on counting butts in seats, punching time clocks, and demanding continual maximum effort. The bottom line is you don't have to follow this unnatural script. Slow down between sprints and do it better—and, provided you get the desired results, do it your way.

Never Criticize Intelligence (Including Your Own)

You're not qualified to judge intelligence. Traditional definitions of intelligence are changing and expanding. You may think you have smart pegged, but you'd likely be wrong. Snapping a chalk line on the intelligence in the room might make you feel better, in control, and accomplished, but it delimits everyone, including you, and diminishes the potential power of the group. I have two older brothers, and they are both very intelligent, each one brilliant in a different way. As a result, they couldn't be more different and rarely talk, I suspect because they struggle to understand one another. While the oldest has cultivated an inherited high IQ, the middle brother has developed a high EQ (emotional quotient) through experiential learning gained largely from time living on the streets. In the spectrum of human information, it's been said that there is, from left to right, *data, information, knowledge,* and *wisdom.* In our world, we are awash in the first two, data and information, while we find knowledge and wisdom less plentiful and more elusive. If anyone were to ask me which of my brothers might move farthest along this information scale achieving wisdom, I would not have bet it would be my middle brother, yet somehow he surpassed all of us, and the reason has to do with ambidexterity. In order to achieve wisdom, one must possess both kinds of intelligence (IQ and EQ). This duo is becoming more important and will become more evident as we move further into the digital and artificial intelligence economies. What is EQ? let's take a closer look.

Develop the New Smart

"My robot boss is kind of insensitive, so I cover for him."

Ed Hess said humility will be the new strength of future leaders.[47] During what Hess called the "smart machine age" (SMA), we must learn to become "new smart." This will entail leveraging increasingly more of our EQ skills, made up of things like *self-awareness, self-regulation, empathy,* and *motivation.* Hess said we cannot compete with machines in terms of processing data and re-taining information, so we will have to either complement the work of machines or do the work they can't do, like critical thinking, emotional engagement, empathy, and creativity. To succeed in the SMA we will need to learn four practices: *quieting ego, managing self, reflective listening,* and *otherness* (establishing connections with

---

[47] Hess, E. (2017). *Humility is the new smart.* https://www.amazon.com/s?k=humility+new+smart&ref=nb_sb_noss

others). We will need to connect emotionally with others and change our mental model from the world that "was" into the world that will be. Hess said humility doesn't mean being weak, and we must learn to slow ourselves down through mindful attention, purposefully noticing moments without judgment, and practice better self-management. Hess added that humanity has created a society hyper focused on individual success, competition, and aggression, leaving us too self-involved and fixed in our beliefs to currently be adept in such skills. We will only excel in the SMA when we collaborate. A new age of cultivated interpersonal skills is dawning; we need to know what our personal skills are and develop them.

Redefine "Best" Every Day

An author I read recently (I'm embarrassed to say I can't remember who) said that we often treat ourselves unfairly by imposing unrealistic expectations about what constitutes our best. They're right. How do we do this? By comparing today's best effort with yesterday's best. The problem with this is today's a different day with different circumstances and yesterday's best may have been unusually good, an "all-time" best. How can you avoid this trap? Replace yesterday's "best" with a new best for today and forget about yesterday.

14

Welcome to Shangri-La:

Organizational Ambidexterity and the Company You Keep

Welcome to Shangri-La, an idyllic paradise of your choosing and design. Of course, no place is 100% perfect; however, we've spent the course of this book discussing, exploring, and determining how close to it we can actually get—and it is possible to get there. I know because I've seen it. If you've read these pages, you can get there too. Happiness begins with a state of mind and ends with you stepping out into the place of your heart's desire.

Too often, we compulsively charge through life acting, and reacting, similar to how we did yesterday, last week, or last year. But we can't solve tomorrow's problems with last week's behavior; we have to engage our brains and step into the clearing in order to see an accurate, connected picture. Let's discuss world views, review what we have discussed, and finish by considering a few tips you can take with you on the road to engineering your perfect life. I've certainly enjoyed our time together.

You and Your Organization's World View

In the book *A Brief History of Thought*, Luc Ferry (pronounced fur-ree') discussed defining moments in Western philosophical thought that have dominated history and subsequently affected the world. These philosophies, and in one case a religion, have influenced our thoughts and activities, whether we give them daily conscious attention or not. Philosophies and faiths such as *stoicism, humanism, postmodernism, Christianity, pragmatism,* and most recently *contemporary humanism,* all Google-able terms by the way, influence our world view (a comprehensive conception of the universe and humanity's relation to it). By virtue of this, our organization's philosophy and world view are also formed. There may be nothing written or spoken about philosophies or world views around your company, but I assure you they are there and have an influence. From everything to the furniture in the lobby to the architecture of the building and the boss's Maserati, clues are everywhere regarding your company's views about work and life. The natural order and flow of ambidextrous organizations, those that can both exploit and explore the marketplace, borrow the best from these philosophies and movements and closely follow the current thinking of the day, *contemporary humanism,* a philosophy Ferry said offers a compelling blend of all the best values that have come before.

Stoicism, Christianity, and Humanism

With *stoicism,* created by the ancient Greeks, humanity was introduced to the idea of logical thought, control of emotions (developing indifference to both pleasure and pain), the view that there is a logical cosmic order to the universe that is external to us and beyond our influence, and the ability to achieve contentment and harmony by following a universal path. Next came *Christianity.* Instead of a predefined universal logical order and reason external to us, humanity was introduced to freedom of choice and the idea we are transient and capable of change. The locus of control had shifted from external (out of our control) to internal (within our influence and control). Furthermore, Christianity, like other religions, espouses a focus on serving humanity as opposed to objects or things. With the scientific revolution in the 16th and 17th centuries, humanity was again pulled back to ideas of universal truths and laws. External control that was out of our hands, insignificance, and impermanence in a big world and the vastness of space must have been an unfathomable and terrifying thought to many. Perhaps to counter this, the philosophy of *humanism* came on the scene. With this, philosopher Jean-Jacques Rousseau set out to reinterpret the scientific revolution with man at the center, having dominion over, or at least control of, himself within its mechanical workings.

Postmodernism and Pragmatism

With each philosophy or belief, the pendulum seems to swing between a rational (logical) and normative (behavioral) approach and between an exploitative (narrowly focusing) and explorative (broadly expanding) focus and thought in a sine wave pattern. Two rational traditions worthy of note are pragmatism and post-modernism. With its emphasis on practical applications of the world's philosophical topics such as nature and the universe, *pragmatism* prescribed the ultimate in logical, practical approaches. In 1907, Harvard Professor William James said pragmatism was perhaps America's greatest contribution to the world. Frederick Nietzsche, German philosopher and architect of the *postmodern era,* taught a philosophy that prescribes focusing on the "here and now" present moment; focusing thought on anything else was a complete waste of time. True ambidextrous organizations naturally borrow the best from the ebb-and-flow pendulum swing that the different philosophies and faiths have collectively produced—in part because they follow in sync with the complexity of life.

Contemporary Humanism and Ambidexterity

Just like structures, values can also be vertical or horizontal. Stoicism, Christianity, and the philosophies discussed here are compilations of beliefs, and each is spread horizontally across humanity or is built up vertically in columns of specific (disassociated from mankind) activities, disciplines, and modes of thought. Borrowing the best from stoicism, Christianity, prag-matism, postmodernism, and particularly humanism, philosophers have arrived at *contemporary humanism,* a new philosophy that incorporates logical rationality and defines spirituality in nonreligious ways for both work and life.

One of the ideas of the contemporary humanist movement is *transcendence*. It comes from postmodern thinking and is illustrated by German philosopher Edmund Husserl and his matchbox analogy. We know that a matchbox has six sides, but when we hold it up to our eyes we can only see three sides at any one time; the other sides of the box are hidden from view, though we conclude they are there. For Husserl, this suggests something interesting: that some things are transcendent, beyond our knowing, in this case visually. What Husserl means is that some parts of reality are unknown; we automatically fill in blank spaces with our minds in the models we build for utility and convenience. However, not everything is seen, and it is important to acknowledge these unknown parts.

This is the way that mental models like paradigms and schema serve us best—as servants for us in building bridges and connections from the known to the unknown and identifying the parts still under construction, and not as our masters telling us unequivocally what is. Ambidextrous organizations operate in the same way. Whether companies are currently exploiting or exploring in the environment, they never assume unseen portions of a business reality are as they have traditionally been. Consequently, they test them with the belief that some things are transcendental and prone to change. Though we may be able to mentally configure a complete reality with confidence from what we can see, that doesn't mean it is concrete. A great many yet unknown details can and do end up being filled in prematurely. Once we become comfortable with the idea that we can never see all our reality at once from our sole and unique perspective, we can train our minds to a new definition of reality that includes an element of the unknown and unseen for exploration. Additionally, under our new definition and paradigm, the presence of one thing implies the absence of something else, and this should be sought out and considered. Under our old paradigm, we would have likely ignored or overlooked such ideas.

Thus, reality depends on the angle of observation; whichever angle we view life from will inform our real and transcendental experience. Husserl has taught us that no matter how we contemplate reality, we can never totally grasp it, and we cannot totally grasp it alone. Ambidextrous organizations have learned that *shared* explorative practices combined with focused exploitation enable them to perform at peak efficiency, imagine more, and shine light into corners individuals alone cannot illuminate.

Husserl's experiment also transfers to other notions such as not assuming all perspectives are the same or that some are better (more valuable or advantageous) than others. Thought, reflection, and problem solving are not linear exercises. What this means is that allocation should be given for time, uncertainty, and figuring things out.

Nietzsche's Active and Reactive Forces

Also from postmodernism comes Frederick Nietzsche's belief that the world is split into opposing active and reactive forces. According to Nietzsche, reactive forces function by denying and repressing other forces. This idea fits with established exploitative organizational practices designed to be followed, repeated, preserved, and protected as originally created. These represent a narrowing of prescribed behavior and thought in the name of efficiency and perfection. Think of a surgeon or aviator following critical checklist steps or a factory worker repeating steps in an assembly line. Were these procedures not followed exactly, the consequences could be dire or costly.

Active forces, by comparison, don't repress other forces, in part because such forces are yet unknown; the focus is on discovery or creation. Active forces open new perspectives and, when done right, attempt to follow as few established pathways as possible. Art and music come to mind as examples of experiences that do not need to prove any other predecessor wrong. As the author put it: "One could not say, for example, that Picasso was wrong and Monet was right." The same idea holds true for free associative thought or any type of exploration, physical or mental. Such trailblazing activities often have little referential precedence, so there should be nothing to honor, oppose, or protect.

Organizational ambidexterity with its opposing exploitative and explorative identities illustrates Nietzsche's idea of an active and reactive world. These behaviors are akin to explorative activities in ambidextrous organizations, in which everything is initially considered when in search of innovation, creative behavior, or exploration. Instead of prescribing one mindset over the other (active or reactive), Nietzsche recommended working toward a balancing of the two, a practice he called a "will to power" and achieving it "the grand style." This balanced, orchestrated dance is choreographed daily by ambidextrous and complexity leaders in the most innovative companies around the world.

Understanding Your Organization's World View

If you don't know what your organization's philosophy and world view is, I encourage you to seek it out. You may discover it has never considered one. All the same, there is one, or several, present. Is your organization more logic and reason or faith based? For Christian-based businesses like Hobby Lobby or Chick-fil-A, it's relatively easy to tell, but not so for other organizations. Look in your company's tenets, value or mission statement, or employee manual or handbook or ask the CEO, and then ask yourself if that answer aligns with yours. Is the world view normative or rational? Is it ambidextrous (exploitative and explorative) and, if so, at what percentages? Is it 90% exploitative and 10% explorative? Or 60%/40%?

Beyond capitalism, humanism, or any other type of "isms" our company may endorse or imply, there is a base desire in all of us to learn, help, contribute, create, and exercise our brain and its right creative/left logic cognitive functions. How much and in what ways we can do this will ultimately determine our happiness and success. Once you discover your organization's philosophy and world view, ask yourself whether that aligns with yours and whether that matters to you.

Jerry Colonna, author of *Reboot*, said that now more than ever, there are "ghosts in the machine"—things that are neither known, expected, or that we readily know what to do about. Combine this with the idea that we are finite, messy, asymmetrical beings and life is not a linear progression, and it points to the idea that we should be comfortable embracing not knowing at work (and life) and do the best we can every day without stressing too much about it. What does Colonna prescribe to cope with a messy, changing, kaleidoscope world? Once you know more about the philosophy and world view of your organization and yourself, try some of these tips from Jerry's book and your life should get smoother and more fulfilling.

- Apply the logic of the do-over like when you were a kid. Activities might take iterations (do-overs) before they're right.
- Shoot, or learn to live with, your crow of self-criticism that endlessly caws at you when you think something hasn't gone exactly right. Remember that although it is critical of you, it's also a part of you that cares (so you may want to reckon with it rather than shoot it).
- Remember that discipline and mental toughness are necessary. Develop both and they will be your champions in exploitative endeavors and defensive tackle during explorative ones.

One final piece of advice comes from Milarepa, a 10th-century Buddhist saint: "Surrender to your demons. Face your fears head on and invite them to do their worst. Do this and you will be rewarded with your freedom."

The Ambidextrous Organization

So, you have been introduced to *organizational ambidexterity*, defined as the ability to simultaneously exploit and explore the marketplace for profit—not an easy thing to do considering the two can appear on the surface as contradictory. For this reason it's no wonder that 40-plus years of research has said that *exploitation drives out exploration.* In other words, when you learn to do something successfully, you mechanize and refine those processes, and you stop looking for new things to discover and do. The underlying message here is that since exploitation drives out exploration, exploitatively inclined people can drive out exploratively inclined people. You may think you have evolved into a high-performing, high-producing company and your spreadsheets and CFO may be touting this line when in reality you may have dismissed your most creative, innovative, courageous, and caring people! Though all companies start ambidextrous, exploring in creative and aggressive ways, few make it past temporal ambidexterity (switching) to achieve structural or contextual ambidexterity like today's most successful companies.

Culture

Next comes culture. Although it may be the most important subject we could discuss, it's a latecomer to the organizational scene, being marginalized and ignored ever since Edgar Schein first coined the phrase "corporate culture" in the 1970s. Yet the words of Schein still ring true today: *"Perhaps the single most important thing a leader does for their organization is set the culture."* Furthermore, I will add, if leaders don't set the culture, they're going to get one anyway and they may not like it or even know what they have. This is a dangerous predicament many organizations find themselves in, and ailments run the gamut from suffering undiagnosed flu-like symptoms for years, never performing at top efficiency, to experiencing a debilitating event that damages the organization. Imagine owning a beautiful Ferrari with no acceleration, in desperate need of a tune up; this is what operating with a damaged culture is like. The smartest companies secretly know that culture is king. As Peter Drucker said, "Culture eats strategy for breakfast."

Bob Chapman, co-author of *Everybody Matters,* whom I've had the pleasure of speaking with, recommends treating each of your employees like family. I'm not talking about treating them to annual baseball tickets, summer picnics, or lavish Christmas parties, but really treating them like family by sincerely listening to them, finding out what they're passionate about, providing stretch and growth opportunities, and physically doing things that say "I care." Get this right and you have a strong, capable, and successful family. Get it wrong, superficially "half-ass" it, or turn a blind eye to forces within your organization that might be sending a counter-cultural message, and you may damage your culture even worse than if you did nothing.

For these reasons, the most important type of culture you can strive for is an ambidextrous one, which encourages creativity and exploitative behavior in an all-inclusive setting. Question in point: Would you kick your conservative, slightly militant uncle or liberal peace-loving nephew out of the family because they get into raucous debates every Thanksgiving over their passionate world views, or would you strive to integrate their unique perspectives into the family's view and turn it towards the family's growth and betterment?

One of my most memorable personal experiences of ambi-dexterity in action and the effect it had on culture happened to me as a young sergeant while stationed in Tucson, Arizona. My squadron, the 41st Electronic Combat Squadron, had a rich military history going as far back as 1917 and the Company "A" 4th Balloon Squadron. Our service included a squadron in Takhli, Thailand, during the Vietnam War and an incident that became the inspiration for the movie *Bat 21*. Our newly minted squadron commander, Lt. Col. Don Bacon, was looking for a subtle yet powerful way to illustrate this rich history for his fellow squadron members. He knew enough about me, a lower-ranking enlisted person under his command, to know that, like him, I was a fan of history and the power it had to add insight and context to the present. Earlier in the year, I had volunteered to take on the ancillary duty of making going-away plaques for squadron members leaving the unit. I had received a framing certification from the base hobby shop, giving me use of their facilities for framing. Col. Bacon asked me if I had an interest in helping research the squadron history and I did, and I knew instantly what I wanted to do. I immediately went to work in my spare time calling the National Archives in Washington, DC, and researching and ordering photographs of every type of aircraft the squadron had ever flown, to include balloons. Some of these photos, regenerated from negatives and microfilm, had not been seen in decades. As the photos began to trickle in, I took them one by one to the framing shop and professionally framed each, lining the halls of the squadron with our amazing history. I even purchased a *Bat 21* movie poster and took it to Lt. Col. Iceal "Gene" Hambleton, the real-life navigator played by actor Gene Hackman. I got him to sign the poster for our squadron ready room (break room). The experience Lt. Col. Bacon's squadron culture allowed me to have gave me the latitude to explore creatively and personally within the bounds of our squadron's mission and responsibilities. This experience, as well as the additional experiences it generated, energized and sustained me, making me more focused, committed, and devoted to my technical duties and our ever-vigilant mission.

An important footnote to this story concerns the ambidextrous leader. The unique mission of our aircraft necessitated a crew complement of two commanders on our planes: an aircraft commander up front flying and a mission crew commander in the back running the mission. Lt. Col. Bacon was the first mission crew commander in the history of the squadron to become group commander as well as wing commander. I suspect the reason for this was because left- and right-brained leadership skills were valued by his superiors. This "whole-brain" perspective continued to serve Don Bacon, as he rose to the rank of Air Force brigadier general during his career and currently serves as U.S. Congressman for Nebraska's second district.

Leadership

Millions of dollars are spent each year on books about leadership. Yet with 1,500 current definitions and over 40 concepts, which is the one true definition, and what are companies using? Ambidextrous organizations use two leadership concepts successfully:

ambidextrous leadership and complexity leadership. The models have similar characteristics, and each comprises three types of leaders—leaders who are helpful, have the heart of a teacher and a student, and have a high level of emotional intelligence.

Learning

If culture is the most important aspect of any organization, then learning runs a very close second. As the original title of my research, "learning in ambidexterity," suggests, the term *ambidextrous organization* is really code for "learning organization." Most organizations practice organizational learning, but few graduate to becoming a learning organization. Ambidextrous organizations are in this cohort. To reach this level, you must let learning happen, accept it in whatever form it shows up, and immediately capture and share it when it does. Learning doesn't always need structure to frame it, and it doesn't use silence. It's not timid and doesn't discriminate, play favorites, or pay homage to anything, unless it's the open mind.

Structure

Structure is important to companies; without it they would be like boneless jellyfish. But with too much structure, they can become rigid and brittle. With that said, there are times when jellyfish have the perfect "structureless" structure to quickly react, getting a unique job done, so what's the right type of structure for a company? The answer depends on what is going on. Ambidextrous organizations don't give in to inertia (cultural or structural); they stay flexible, pivot easily, and keep several types of structure (horizontal and vertical, for example) in their "back pocket" for every opportunity or situation.

Complexity

Albert Einstein said, "Everything should be as simple as possible but no simpler." Einstein was right. Just because the world is complex doesn't mean it has to be complicated. Just a little understanding of complexity science and complex adaptive systems can go a long way in helping you understand and navigate your business world. Neuroscience, biology, and physics are all sciences that help to explain and inform the humanity of business. Language creates frameworks that allow us to make sense out of our world, and since the beginning of the industrial revolution organizations have explained and understood the business world using the language of Newtonian physics. The descriptive language we have used for the last two and a half centuries to create our work realities has been anchored in the language of *cause and effect, predictability,* and *certainty;* it's a world of distinct wholes and their parts. A reality drawn from Newton is one of the observable world, quantifiable determinism, linear thinking, and a controllable, slow-moving future with expected outcomes. The business world of today, by contrast, is much different from that of 250 years ago.

It's time to add a new operating language into our thinking and mental models, one built on the language of quantum physics. Quantum physics largely revised Newton's classical view, giving us a more refined picture of reality. The world of quantum physics is different because it is a world rich in relationships considered at the "subatomic" level. It is a world of *discrete events, emergence, complexity, fractals, relationships between objects,* and *weak linkages.* Quantum physics also invites discussions of other phenomena and theories like *chaos theory, order* and *change, autonomy* and *control.* Bottom line: Applying quantum physics provides a more refined and detailed picture of business and the effect it has on your workforce.

The Brain

It's been said that we live simultaneously on two planes of existence: the observable physical world and the world inside our heads. The reality of life that we experience is a reconciliation of the two. The mind is a funny thing; it craves structure and at the same time resists it. It experiences synchronous events, flow, and intuitive and rational thought, often preferring one or the other. Organizational ambidexterity, the ability to behave in both exploitative and explorative ways, allows and encourages left, right, and whole-brain thinking.

Wellness and the Authentic Self

Living our best life, at work and home, and being our authentic selves are the highest and most rewarding achievements we could reach in life. But how do we keep peace of mind and keep our natural defenses in check in such a crazy, chaotic world and with such crazy, chaotic minds? In ambidextrous organizations, it's easier to find and be your authentic self, as there is more of a chance that you will be valued not just for your skill sets, but also for the person you are, no matter how different that might be from your coworkers. The bottom line is you won't have to hide because you're different. Diversity is not just a valued asset in an ambidextrous organization; it's a strength and expectation.

Arriving

How will you know when you're part of an ambidextrous organization where you could realize the full range of your potential and become the person you most want to be? You'll know because you will not only be allowed but also encouraged to behave as your authentic, and maybe ambidextrous (exploitative and explorative), self. Arriving at an ambidextrous organization is arriving at a learning organization, learning in real time as it grows and adapts. Learning does not take a back seat to performance; they share equal places at the table. It's also an organization that values and leverages diversity—of thought, of experience, and of age, gender, and ethnicity. It's not timid and sees a red flag if solutions are routinely arrived at quickly, there's always a collegial atmosphere and high camaraderie, and everyone looks and acts the same. Contention, positive deviance, disagreements, and debates are all healthy, growing, breakthrough experiences. Finally, ambidextrous organizations don't make excuses for their people, but they do make concessions for low-energy days, learning curves, mistakes, and second chances, like any healthy family would. It's a tough space but a safe space where ignorance is forgiven but not apathy, and energy is leveraged for creative innovation, productivity, and work.

Some Final Advice

Here's some final advice regarding your behavior and managing the amazing quantum computer between your ears. Do these things and keep yourself productive, healthy, and on your best path.

Channel Your Inner Scientist

One way to develop the ambidextrous mind is to channel your inner scientist. We all conduct "empiric" research, whether we realize it or not; *empiric* simply means observation. We observe the world around us, compare what we see against judgments we've previously made, either validating or invalidating our original thoughts, and move on to the next experience. Don't take yourself too seriously, however, because this type of research is only half-done if not followed up by a healthy dose of deductive reasoning. (Sherlock Holmes would thank you for it.) To put it another way, once you form a hypothesis (an explanation) about something you see, do, hear, or think, you must then put in an equal amount of effort to disprove it, rather than simply believing it and then going about looking for more thoughts to validate and confirm the brilliant thought you just had.

Recently, a colleague suggested my writing reminded him of the work of the late Karl Popper, a critic of the inductivist scientific method. I confessed I had not heard of Popper and, after researching him, became immediately humbled. If I were to channel my inner Popper, or Holmes, I would strongly warn against exclusive inductive thinking. In an article on changing perceptions, Ozan Varol said that changing others' minds, and our own, can be a tricky thing because the mind doesn't just follow facts. It also follows emotions and protects itself using things like confirmation bias (looking for more "like" things to strengthen its case), *under-valuing* evidence that contradicts its beliefs and *overvaluing* evidence that confirms what it likes. What Ozan doesn't say but alludes to is that in order to influence, one must reach not only the rational side of the mind but also the intuitive, feeling side. Simply spewing out facts to change a person's perspective is no better in the end than spewing obscenities at someone and may have the same effect: you'll just piss them off.

Neuroscientist Rudy Tanzi would have agreed with Popper, saying, "Your only job as a scientist should be to disprove your current theory, taking the threads of truth you have learned from your last defunct theory and sewing them into your next, new, updated theory, which you then try to disprove anew." How much better would organizations and humanity be if we consciously practiced this kind of iterative thinking in all we did?

How can you break the confirmation bias trap of making assumptions about things and then looking for supporting data, ignoring everything else? We must change the processes of our mind and our reactive compulsive thoughts in order to change behavior. It's a chain reaction. The minute we attempt to cut corners by *prematurely* reducing, limiting, or deselecting possibilities, we lock ourselves into fewer and fewer possible selections. It may feel satisfying in the moment to say you're done early, but why do it if a decision doesn't have to be made or an action doesn't have to be immediately taken? Is it a responsible, smart, and best decision for the group? What's the right answer? Unless there's a grizzly bear charging you at the water cooler, you don't need to make imme-diate decisions or take immediate action. Suspend judgment until a decision must be made. You may encounter valuable, new last-minute insights. Organizations could have these watershed mo-ments more often if they shared their daily empirical research. Self-awareness should be a team activity!

According to Ian McGilchrist,[48] the left hemisphere of the brain (our rational side) has the advantage of perfection because it operates in a closed system, arguing for and advocating only that which is known. As a result, the argument of the left brain is a polished, convincing one, as it shaves off everything from its model that doesn't fit. This left hemisphere mind is a formidable asset provided it has the necessary answers to make a good decision, but the left hemisphere thinks in the immediate, the literal, and the tactical. By contrast, the right hemisphere doesn't have as convincing a voice, as it prefers to deal with the unknown, the abstract, and the intuitive. How does this play out in the social and organizational world? Think of the old TV show *All in the Family*, and if you've never seen an episode of this groundbreaking sitcom, it's suggested viewing.

Know How You Think

Daniel Kahneman in his book *Thinking Fast and Slow* said there is a compelling drama taking place in the human mind because we think in two different ways. One way is in a state of "cognitive ease" (he calls this System 1), while the other is in a state of "cognitive strain" (labeled System 2). So, we have an impulsive, automatic, intuitive System 1 side and a thoughtful, deliberate, and calculating System 2 side. Their interactions determine how we think, with 2 equaling conscious activities and 1, unconscious activities. The human mind is woefully and efficiently lazy. Because the mind is an energy hog, consuming as much as 25% of our body's energy, it prefers to save energy by following familiar preconstructed "deer paths" of thought and decision making whenever possible rather than blazing new trails. Operating exclusively in System 1 can create errors when a problem is perceived as simpler than it is. More than 70% of our waking day is executed on autopilot. System 1 will call on System 2 when faced with a problem it can't figure out but will not call upon it if it perceives the problem as simple, as it would require more energy to

---

[48] McGilchrist, I. (2011). *The divided brain*. https://www.youtube.com/watch?v=dFs9WO2B8uI

do so. Thinking and processing are conservatively done "on the cheap" whenever possible, passing by System 1 thinking first to see if the problem can be resolved there before settling on the slower and costlier System 2.

For this reason, the human mind has created a "cheat sheet" of shortcuts it uses to save resources. The result? Sometimes we get things done faster and more efficiently, but when we use these shortcuts we are not always in conscious control of our actions, judgments, and choices and we make mistakes. What are these helpful shortcuts and how can they sometimes "dis-serve" us? We already discussed a few. Let's look at a few more taken from *Thinking Fast and Slow*, being aware of how these could help us when they are encountered.

Common Tricks of the Mind[49]

Priming. We are constantly being primed when exposure to words, concepts, or events causes us to summon related words and concepts in our thinking and actions, and this priming happens completely unconsciously. As an example, you can be primed with the idea of money prior to participating in an event, and this can influence your behavior away from altruism and collaborative cooperation and towards one of individual competition and self-centeredness (selfishness). In another example, subjects primed with words that invoked images of senior citizens such as "Florida," "wrinkle," and "retirement" responded by walking slower than usual. Priming affects the way in which we think and act, and this reflects back into our culture and decisions.

Halo effect. Through this "exaggerated emotional coherence," we tend to oversimplify things without enough information, which can lead to judgment errors. For example, we learn one favorable thing about someone or something, and as a result we like everything about them. The halo effect occurs because our mind wants to

---

[49] Kahneman, D. (2011). *Thinking fast and slow.* https://www.amazon.com/Thinking-Fast-Slow-Daniel-Kahneman/dp/0374275637/ref=tmm_hrd_swatch_0?_encoding=UTF8&qid=1566 580063&sr=8-3

make quick judgments about things, but usually we don't have enough data to make an accurate call.

Heuristics. Our mind continually looks for shortcuts. One type of heuristic shortcut is substitution—when your mind answers (substitutes) an easier question for the more difficult one originally posed. An example would be if someone asked if a particular woman would make a good choice for sheriff. Your mind may substitute this question with a much easier one: whether she looks like she would make a good sheriff. This heuristic means that instead of researching her qualifications, you instead ask yourself the easier question of whether this candidate matches your mental image of a sheriff. Heuristics are usually helpful; however, they are often overused or applied to situations for which they are not suited.

Base rate. We ignore statistical data because we prefer our own expectations over facts. Suppose you received data that said 80% of a city's taxis were blue and 20% were yellow. That would make the base rate for blue taxis 80% and the base rate for yellow taxis 20%. However, you are more familiar with and prefer yellow taxis. If you were to then order a cab, chances are it would be blue. If you then saw five blue cabs go by, you may begin to think it's time you should see a yellow one. However, the base rate stats say you are likely to continue to see blue cabs. Remember the base rate when predicting an event, not your expectations or what you favor.

A Few Final Tips from Me

Put a high value on your time. Be generous, gracious, and act with humility, but realize your time is just as valuable as everyone else's. Be selective and protective of it. Look for time opportunities that pay the most dividends, and when you give your time, give it all.

Get into the fray. Put yourself out there and take a chance. Years ago, as a sergeant in the Air Force, I applied for a special-duty assignment flying as a crewmember aboard Air Force II. Not like regular Air Force assignments, Presidential Airlift was a duty that involved a comprehensive interview process in a cattle call mass hiring event that occurred once every year and a half. The best and brightest airmen from military bases around the world would compete for these coveted jobs during a weeklong event. I honestly didn't know if I was good enough to compete with such athletes in this arena, but I was compelled to swallow my fear and try.

With my formal package submitted, reviewed, and accepted, I was selected for an interview. I couldn't be more excited. Two weeks before the date arrived, however, I received a call informing me that due to a squadron accounting error they would not be able to fly me out for the interview during the current cycle. I would have to reapply during the next interview cycle more than a year away. I was crestfallen; it's all I wanted to do.

Eventually the disappointment faded and I settled back into my old job, consciously forgetting my aspirations, when one day 2 months later my squadron commander approached me with a request. We had to ferry one of our EC-130 aircraft from Arizona to a little Navy base in Southern Maryland and drop it off for testing, and he wanted to know if I would be his flight engineer for the trip. We could fly back commercial. Without hesitation I said yes. The following week, after delivering the plane in Maryland, I jumped in a rental car and drove straight to Andrews Air Force Base. Stopping at the Burger King on base, I called my Air Force II contact I had submitted my package to, telling him I was in town (on base) and asking if we could meet. Momentarily hesitant, trying to get his head around the idea that I had traveled to Maryland unexpectedly, he asked me if I could get some breakfast and call him back in an hour. "One last thing" he asked before hanging up, "Do you happen to have your service dress 'blue's' uniform with you?" "Yes," I said, "I have it in the trunk of the car." When I called back an hour later, he asked if I could come over to the squadron after lunch. He had arranged an interview board to meet exclusively with me.

I was hired that afternoon and welcomed into the squadron with handshakes and claps on the shoulder, and the interview board members told me three things that day. First, they said, no one had ever knocked on their front door and asked for a job. Second, no one had ever spent their own money to come out for an interview. And lastly, if I had interviewed in their mass hiring event, I may not have been hired. They told me I didn't fit the profile of the people they were accustomed to seeing. I would likely have been overshadowed and overlooked. Because of the type A personalities they had come to expect, they most likely would have missed me.

The 6 years I spent at the 99th Airlift Squadron (until my retirement) were the best years of my Air Force career. Being part of a high-performing team where each member focused on the success of their fellow members, safely delivering our nation's leaders to destinations around the world, and being a part of history was the experience of a lifetime and one I will never forget. It changed and improved me forever. Stretch yourself, do something you don't feel ready to do, and go for what you want.

Suspend judgment and delay decisions until they must be made. Many of us want and feel we need to make decisions early. Whether it's anxiety, fear, or something else that motivates us, we want to know how we feel early and lock things down. Life doesn't always work that way, and sometimes that's good; make the decision when it's time.

Be helpful or don't be there. Wherever you find yourself each day, be helpful. If you find that you can't or won't, quietly remove yourself.

Replace assumptions with questions. Often we would rather assume than question; it's easier and often less messy. The problem with this is that assumptions can accumulate. Too many assumptions and we may find ourselves at the end of a long decision tree of our own creation living in an alternate universe by ourselves.

Review old tapes. From my training as a certified hypnotherapist, I know we draw much of our daily behavior from prerecorded tapes; some neuroscientists say it is up to 70%. These tapes, or scripts, were written long ago and are the sign of an intelligent, efficiently operating mind. Designed to do all sorts of things, from streamline repetitive processes, keep us safe from harm or humiliation, or make us more efficient, they are for the most part helpful. The problem with these tapes, however, is that sometimes they're outdated and obsolete, and we may not even realize they're no longer appropriate. After all, you're not 11 anymore. Review and rewrite.

My hope is that you have enjoyed this book and will find it useful as you move through life. A friend recently reviewing my writing on organizational ambidexterity said in a slightly annoyed tone, "You should be writing about something else." His chief complaint? I was in danger of pigeonholing myself by continuing to write about one subject, ambidexterity. What my very smart (slightly left-brained) friend will eventually come to realize is that what I have been writing about all along has been how to create our best world from the elements we have around us.

Dr. Zabiegalski is available to talk to your organization or venue about this groundbreaking research or speak informatively and eloquently about organizational culture, leadership, strategy, learning, complexity, neuroscience in business, creativity, mindfulness, talent management, personal success, emotional intelligence, and action learning.

Contact Eric about a talk or help today.

CPSIA information can be obtained
at www.ICGtesting.com
Printed in the USA
BVHW011843251119
564778BV00005B/93/P

9 781646 333417